FITZWARREI

THE LITIGATION HANDBOOK

A Guide to the Civil Courts

Alan Matthews

© Fitzwarren Publishing 1995

Published by
Fitzwarren Publishing,
PO Box 6887,
London N19 2TR

ISBN 0 9524812 2 7

A CIP record for this book is available from the British Library

Printed and bound by UTL Ltd, London W1

Alan Matthews is a pseudonym

CONTENTS

PREFACE

I had originally intended this book to be a guide purely for litigants in person. After all there are considerable numbers of people conducting their own litigation in the courts and as far as I am aware there is no other book which is directed specifically to them. Legal textbooks with a few honourable exceptions, do little to make themselves accessible to those who might want to consult them. They assume a degree of expertise and familiarity with terminology that many, including lawyers, may not possess. The standard and semi-official civil procedure guides, used by practically every lawyer, certainly every litigator, are the worst offenders. To find one's way around these, particularly the *Supreme Court Practice* or "*White Book*", never mind to be able to understand and apply the contents, is a considerable feat in itself.

As I worked on the book the idea that I could write it "off the top of my head" was quickly shown to be a ridiculous presumption. Much I had to look up. That which I could write without researching generally constituted things I had learnt through my years of practice: much of it learnt very much the hard way. A guide to tell me the things every lawyer is presumed to know would have most helpful when I was starting out at the Bar.

Therefore although I hope this book will have a value for non-lawyers, whether actually involved in conducting litigation or just a curious by-stander, I believe that it may also assist many who earn their living in the courts.

The term "user-friendly" may be unattractive jargon, but it is a concept that legal publishers should have far more regard to. Hence I have tried to produce a book that is exactly that. Should readers think that I have fallen into the trap of presupposing knowledge, in respect of which I berate others, I should be grateful for comments telling me where.

For reasons I explain in detail in the preface to the *Landlords' & Tenants' Handbook* I use the masculine throughout when describing a hypothetical purpose. I am not entirely comfortable adopting this sexist use of language, but on balance it is preferable to any of the alternatives.

Deciding what to exclude to keep the book succinct has been a more significant worry. Not all types of cases can be covered. I concentrate on common law disputes. These represent the majority of matters to come before the courts. They are generally the less complicated form of litigation. Wills and trusts I only touch in the barest of outline. Family matters, important though they are, I have decided to leave altogether, hopefully for another author in the same series. Likewise employment cases. These for the most part are now dealt with in industrial tribunals. These tribunals have a different, and simpler procedure, to the general courts. That too is more profitably dealt with in a separate work. The other numerically significant area that does not fit in with the bulk of discussion in this book is possession cases. There are overlaps with the procedures dealt with in this book, and·the whole area of landlord and tenant law I have already dealt with in another book in this series. As for the courts, it is the county court on which I concentrate. Again for the simple reason that the vast majority of litigation within the capability of an unqualified person or an inexperienced lawyer will be conducted in that court rather than the High Court.

The book deals only with English and Welsh law (which are synonymous). Northern Irish and Scottish law have their overlaps, but it would be inadvisable to rely on a work such as this particularly in Scotland.

As I have been writing three developments have occurred that affect the subject matter of the book. The Regulations permitting solicitors to accept cases on the basis that they will only be paid if successful have been introduced; the Lord Chancellor has produced a Green Paper proposing fundamental "reforms" to the legal aid system, and most significantly of all the Woolf Report *Access to Justice* has been published. I have been able to incorporate all three into the text in so far as was appropriate. So significant is the Woolf Report that I have dedicated a special section to it. Generally I have aimed to state the law as it stood on 1 September 1995.

1. INTRODUCTION: USING THIS BOOK

Examples of cases

The examples in this book are based around three of the commonest types of claim.

The first is Ms Black's claim is against Mr Brown for an unpaid bill for plumbing services. Nothing has been said by Mr Brown to suggest that he is not paying it because he is unhappy with the quality of the work. It is used as a straight-forward example of an unpaid debt.

The second is Mrs Green's claim is against Mr Blue, a shopkeeper, for what she claims is a defective washing machine that she bought from him. She wants her money back and compensation for the damage caused to the clothes in it and surrounding decoration when it overheated. Mr Blue claims that the machine overheated because she overloaded it and that she has only paid half of the agreed price. An outline of the law relating to disputes such as this is contained in chapter 14.

The third example is Mr White's claim is against Ms Fawn. He claims that he was injured when she drove into him as he was walking across a pedestrian crossing. She says that he wasn't on the pedestrian crossing, only near it, and stepped out in such a way that she could do nothing avoid him. An outline of the law relating to such disputes is contained in chapter 13.

Nomenclature, Court Rules, Law Reports and statutes

When using words or phrases that have a specific meaning in the legal context I have put them in italics. Those which are the result of idiom rather than quasi-official usage I have also put in inverted commas. Many are also defined in the glossary.

In the footnotes there appear a number of Order numbers. Most of these are the *County Court Rules*, which are abbreviated to *CCR*. Where *RSC* proceeds a rule that indicates it is a *Rule of the Supreme Court* which applies primarily in the High Court, though many also have effect which applies primarily in the High Court, though many also have effect in the county court. These Rules are published in the *County Court Practice* (known as the "*Green Book*") and the *Supreme Court Practice* (known as the "*White Book*") respectively. The *Green Book* is published annually in May, the *White Book* in the November of every even numbered year.

Statutes and case names I also keep to the footnotes. In accordance with standard usage case names are italicised. The reference that follows them is from the law reports. The official Law Reports are used where possible. These are published every week in the Weekly Law Reports. At the end of the year these reports are compiled in to three volumes. This does not mean as logically one would expect that those from January to around April go into volume 1 and so on. Volume 1 consists of the cases that are considered by the editors of the Reports the less important. Volumes 2 and 3 comprise the other cases. Each weekly issue therefore contains a part 1 and either a part 2 or 3 depending on how late on in the year it is. The volume 2 and 3 cases are published in the Law Reports which are divided into Appeal Cases (abbreviated to "AC") for House of Lords cases, Queens Bench ("QB")[1], Chancery ("Ch") and Family ("Fam"). Sometimes there may be more than one volume of any of these reports published in any one year. Almost equal in respectability to the Law Reports are the *All England Law Reports* ("All ER's"). Most cases in these reports are also in the Law Reports and vice versa. There are also specialist reports such as the *Criminal Appeal Reports*, the *Property & Compensation Reports* and the *Lloyd's List Reports* (commercial cases). Most of the quality newspapers publish daily law reports in summary form. *The Times'* are the longest established and most highly regarded.

Further information on legal sources is provided in Chapter 16.

---

[1] The Queen's Bench is of course the *King's Bench* when the monarch is a man, the reports *KB*.

2. PRELIMINARY CONSIDERATIONS

Whether to Litigate

The purpose of litigation is to achieve an end: usually for the plaintiff the payment of money to him by the defendant; and for the defendant the avoidance of that payment. Court proceedings are often and quite sensibly regarded as a last resort. However there are circumstances where they should be commenced at a relatively early stage of a dispute. If one is, say, trying to collect payment of a bill and routine reminders are being ignored, there may be little to be gained by merely sending more reminders. A person cannot have any legitimate complaint if after the second reminder, which incorporated a threat of court proceedings, he is actually sued. Of course he is unlikely to give his custom to the person suing him again, but that may well not constitute much of a loss. Often the costs of commencing proceedings are no more than those of instructing a debt collection agency.

The main consideration in any decision about suing someone has to be whether or not that person is good for the money claimed. There is very little benefit in having a judgement against someone who owns no property and lives on social security: it simply isn't enforceable. Even if the prospective defendant is a little better off than that, extracting money from him is likely to be a lengthy process, which may cost more than can ever be recovered. On the other hand if that person does have the money and appears to have no reason for disputing the claim, taking him to court is far more likely to be a profitable exercise.

Similarly in cases where it is not a simple debt but damages that are being claimed, if the other person doesn't indicate that he is willing to talk about a settlement, there is little to be gained from repeated efforts to make him do so. Insurance companies may have a policy of refusing to pay out to third parties[2], particularly ones not represented by a

---

[2] The term *third party* derives from the insured person being the first party and the insurer the second. The third party is in an insurance context the person injured by the first person and who has a claim against him.

solicitor, unless they issue proceedings. In a case where the claim is virtually indisputable there is nothing to lose by starting a court claim at any early stage.

The real danger in starting such a claim, particularly if it is for more than £1,000, only arises if it fails. Then it is likely that the person who brought the action will have to pay the other side's legal costs[3].

Without prejudice and *Calderbank* letters

Letters written by laypeople about contentious matters are often headed "without prejudice". The words are much misused: sometimes people even use them when writing to their own solicitors. They are appropriate only in relation to negotiations. What they mean is that what is said in the letter should not be used in evidence if the case does go to court. To take Mrs Green's case (introduced on page 9), Mr Blue might write to her after she has made her claim known to him:

> **I totally refute your claim. The machine was working perfectly except that you overloaded it. I am therefore not prepared to agree a refund or pay anything else.**

A "without prejudice" heading would be pointless: he has not made any offer to resolve the dispute. If the words were used and subsequently Mr Blue changed his mind and decided that his defence was that the machine had not been properly installed, the use of the words "without prejudice" would not prevent the court looking at the letter to show his inconsistency.

On the other hand if Mr Blue wrote:

> **I am prepared to offer you the cost of the machine in full and final settlement but I will not pay anything for the cost of the clothes you say were damaged or the redecoration.**

Then the letter should be headed "without prejudice". He has made a

---

[3] The principles on which costs orders are made are discussed on pages 94 to 97.

genuine concession. If people knew the offering of such concessions could be used against them in court, they would be more reluctant to make them. The settlement of claims by negotiation is generally considered to be a good thing: if nothing else it saves the courts' time. Allowing people to make offers in this way encourages such negotiation.

A variation of a without prejudice letter is the *Calderbank*[4] letter. This is a without prejudice letter with the express reservation that it can in due course be shown to the trial judge after the has made his main decision. It will then relevant to the question of costs. If an offer of settlement made in a *Calderbank* letter is not subsequently "beaten" by the person to whom it is addressed, it is likely that that person will not be awarded his legal costs.

Calderbank letters are appropriate both before and after an action commences, if what is being claimed is other than just a single payment of money. When such an amount is being claimed- as it is in all three of the examples given- the correct procedure after the action has commenced is for the defendant to pay money into court, a procedure which is discussed on pages 60 and 61.

Were Mr Blue to make a *Calderbank* offer before Mrs Green commences her action, he might add a few words to his "without prejudice" letter.

> **This letter is intended to be without prejudice except as to costs. Please treat it as a *Calderbank* letter.**

Although generally it is not a good idea for laypeople to use legal phrases, this is one situation where, if used correctly, the expression might show the other side they are up against someone who has some legal knowledge, which could discourage them from litigating.

The letter before action

Before actually commencing an action it is normal practice to write a formal *letter before action*. This should basically say, "Unless you pay

---

[4] After the case of *Calderbank v Calderbank* [1976] Fam 93

up (in the case of a debt) or make me a reasonable offer (in the case c a damages claim) by (say fourteen days after the date of the letter), will sue you in the county court".

Specifying a particular county court always makes the threat sound little more convincing. It is a better to give a particular date as . deadline rather than "within fourteen days". It is not usual for it b headed "without prejudice". However if it contains an offer to settle fo less than will be sued for the words "without prejudice" should be incorporated in the text just before that offer.

Letters before action are of course often sent as a bluff by people who have no intention of suing. For that reason they are not always very effective as a threat. Once a letter before action has been sent and the deadline expired it is highly unlikely that anything other than actually commencing the action will bring about the desired result.

Ms Black's letter to Mr Brown (that example also being explained on page 9) might read:

> **I have already sent two reminders in addition to the bill for the £1,463 you owe me. These you have ignored. You have not returned my many phone calls about the debt. In the circumstances, unless I have received full payment by 28 September 1995, I shall have no choice but to commence proceedings in the Northampton County Court.**
>
> **You will appreciate that if I do this I will incur further costs, which ultimately you will have to bear.**

Negotiation

Unless a claim is completely spurious, the person against whom it is made would be well advised to try to settle it at the earliest possible opportunity. Often this is best done over the telephone rather than in correspondence. If a mutually agreeable figure can be arrived at, it is vital to send it accompanied by a letter containing words to the effect that it is, "Offered in full and final settlement of all claims you may have against me and not otherwise".

Simply ignoring a person's claim is not only grossly discourteous, it makes it very difficult to rely on any defence if the matter does go to court. The question, "If what you now say is right, why didn't you say so when you were first being asked for the money?" is a virtually impossible one to answer. It is only in the criminal law that there has ever been a "right to silence": the civil courts are allowed to draw common sense inferences from people's failure to respond to allegations.

Conversely though, if a person has provided a reason why he is not prepared to pay a bill, merely sending him that bill time and time again without entering into any dialogue about his reasons is counter-productive. If Mr Brown had written to Ms Black saying he wasn't prepared to pay her bill because none of the radiators she had fitted worked, she would be expected to have taken issue with this as soon as she had his letter. A response as to why her work was unsatisfactory that appears for the first time after proceedings have commenced is deeply unconvincing.

Alternative Dispute Resolution

In the last two or three years the concept of *alternative dispute resolution* (ADR) has attracted much attention in the legal press. This basically involves the settling of disputes amicably but with formalised assistance, rather than through having a trial. Ever since litigation began compromise has been possible and desirable. Ideally from the litigants' points of view it should occur by negotiation before lawyers ever become involved in the case at all. ADR in the formal sense however is aimed at resolving matters with lawyers acting for both sides. Sometimes it can be done by a meeting between the parties and their solicitors, maybe with barristers present too. An independent mediator may be asked to chair this meeting. That mediator may act in the capacity of a judge, though without the power to make a binding decision. He can indicate to the parties what he thinks the likely outcome of the case will be, either after having merely read the papers or as a result of hearing submissions from both sides. A number of retired judges and experienced barristers are available to do this type of work[5].

This form of resolution is more likely to succeed in a case which is

---

[5] CEDR, on 0171 430 1852 or ADR Group Ltd, on 0171 925 2090, should be able to assist in providing mediators.

legally complex but where the parties are not accusing each other o
lying. If it does succeed, it will save them much of the money tha
would be spent on a contested trial. However it is not a cheap proces
in itself. The mediator will charge a substantial fee. The parties' lawyer.
will charge for their time preparing for and attending the meeting. It i:
only likely to be productive in a case where both parties are prepared tc
take a common sense view of the merits of their cases. If a persor
attends an ADR meeting convinced that the mediator is going to advise
the other party to give him everything he wants, then he probabl}
shouldn't be going at all!

Ombudsmen

A number of service industries are subject to *ombudsmen* schemes that
enable disputes between them and consumers to be resolved relatively
simply. Banks, building societies and insurance companies all subscribe
to such schemes. There are limits to the type of matters that the
ombudsman can consider. The Banking Ombudsman will not rule on a
matter of the bank's commercial judgement, such as a decision to refuse
a loan; the Insurance Ombudsman cannot deal with third party claims.
From the point of view of the customer these schemes have the
advantage that an unsatisfactory decision is binding only on the
organisation. If the Insurance Ombudsman rules that an insurance
company was entitled to refuse to pay out money when a claim has been
made, it is theoretically open to the insured person to make the same
claim in the courts. A more important advantage may be that they do not
charge the customer any fee and that the decision is made purely on a
consideration of the papers, without anyone needing to actually attend
before the ombudsman.

The ombudsmen will only entertain claims after all the internal
procedures of the organisation have been exhausted. The organisations
are obliged to provide on request details about how claims to their
business's ombudsman are made.

Arbitration schemes

Some trade bodies, such as Association of British Travel Agents (ABTA) and the Motor Agents' Association, offer arbitration when there is a dispute between one of their members and a customer. Unlike the ombudsmen these do require the payment of a fee by the customer. Usually the fee is a little less than would need to be paid to start the case in court. From the customers' point of view there is probably little advantage or disadvantage in using such arbitration. The arbitrator, although appointed by the association, will be a lawyer and probably have a special qualification in arbitration. He is highly unlikely to be biased in favour of the trader. On the other hand travel agents and garages are likely to be familiar with the form of these arbitrations and able to conduct them more confidently than they could if the matter went to court. Sheer bloodymindedness may then persuade some dissatisfied customers to resort to the courts rather than these arbitrations.

Whether or not to instruct a solicitor

A lot of litigation is perfectly within the capability of an intelligent layman, some is not. The county court procedure for claims under £1,000[6], sometimes known as the *small claims court*, is designed to encourage litigants in person. Most of the procedural rules that deal with matters such as exchange of documents and the preparing of witness statements in advance, do not apply to these claims. Legal costs will not as a rule be awarded to the winner in such a case, so it is likely that the solicitor's bill will eat up a fair proportion of the money the winner recovers in damages. In larger claims the fear of having to pay the other side's legal costs sometimes encourages a party to make an offer of settlement once his opponent instructs a solicitor. This is unlikely to happen in a small claim.

Where a remedy other than the payment of money is sought, for instance an injunction or an order that a jointly owned property be sold, the procedure tends to be much more complicated and there are

---

[6] This figure is likely to be raised to £3,000, probably by the end of 1995

considerable advantages in using a solicitor. There are less procedural hoops for the *defendant*, the person being sued, to go through than the *plaintiff*, the person bringing the action. In most disputes it is for the plaintiff to prove his case, and the responsibility is for him to set in motion the court at various stages of the action. The defendant is able to take a more passive role, which can often be done without the aid of legal representation.

Most judges will go out of their way at trial to help litigants in person. They will usually ask questions of any witness that they feel a lawyer would have asked on behalf of that party had he been represented. If there are any points of law that might help that party's case, they may look them up, or require the lawyer representing the other side do so even if it is against his own client's interest. Many lawyers feel that litigants in person actually have an advantage for this reason: the judge in going out of his way to think of every point that might help the litigant in person ends up taking his side. This view is probably something of an exaggeration. A judge can only take points based on the information given to him. It may well be that the litigant in person doesn't state something in court because he doesn't think it is of any importance. The law does sometimes work in mysterious ways and what may seem unimportant to the uninitiated can in fact be crucial. Being legally represented is an advantage for that reason. The eloquent lawyer is probably overrated though. Professional judges are rarely swayed by oratory, though it can be remarkably effective in front of juries.

At some points though legal representation is virtually indispensable. An appeal should never be undertaken without the benefit of an objective experienced opinion as to whether it has any chance of success. Certain injunctions such as *Mareva* and *Anton Piller's* are in practice only granted to be people who appear through solicitors and barristers.

Legal aid

Legal aid, the "*Lucozade*" as lawyers sometimes rather ungratefully refer to it, is a form of assistance to people who become involved in

---

[7] In some actions the terms *applicant* and *respondent* are used rather than *plaintiff* and *defendant* and divorce is sought by the *petitioner*.

litigation. A person litigating without the benefit of legal aid is usually and entirely accurately referred to as "paying privately". It is administered by the Legal Aid Board.

The availability of legal aid is subject to two conditions: the existence of a suitably strong case and lack of financial resources. As a general rule if the solicitor who is initially consulted thinks there is a reasonable case that will be sufficient. In more complicated cases a barrister's opinion may be sought before the suitability of the case for legal aid is finally determined. Sometimes it will be granted up until a certain stage in the action, perhaps the exchange of documents, and then reviewed. Usually the solicitor will have to seek authorization before doing more than a certain amount of work, perhaps £2,500's worth. Other than these restrictions the solicitor, once legal aid has been granted, is free to take any step in the action that a solicitor acting privately might do. The test the Legal Aid Board uses in deciding whether a case is sufficiently strong is to ask whether a person of limited means paying privately would be well-advised to pursue the action. In other words, if someone would be wasting their own money, why should the state pay for it? Legal aid is not available for defamation actions nor currently for tribunals, though it may be extended to cover these in the near future.

Financial eligibility has been cut back considerably in the last decade: very much in keeping with the government's philosophy of reducing public expenditure and services. A further restriction on its availability has been proposed in a Green Paper by the Lord Chancellor. He wants to impose an overall limit on how much is paid out in any one financial year. This could have the effect that once the budget has been exhausted for a particular year, other cases however deserving and urgent may have to be rejected. At the time of writing it is not possible to say how likely to become law this proposal is. However lawyers do have a very good track record of opposing government reforms which may harm their interests. Barristers are better represented in Parliament than any other profession.

People above a certain income or capital level have to pay a contribution. The 1995/96 lower income limit was £2,425, below which no contribution was payable, above £7,187 legal aid would not be available at all. Savings of more than £3,000 would mean some contribution was payable and above £6,750 would mean total ineligibility. In personal injury cases the upper limits are increased by about 10%. If the applicant is a pensioner, the capital limits are considerably relaxed.

The contribution will normally be paid by monthly instalments. The relevant levels are frequently altered. From the income figure expenditure which relates to matters such as housing and travel to work can be disregarded.

Further if a legally aided person wins the case, the Legal Aid Board will have to be paid back out of any money recovered or preserved in those proceedings. This is known as the *statutory charge*. It should be explained both orally and in writing by the solicitor at the time legal aid is granted.

Supposing a litigant claims £5,000 damages and succeeds in his claim with the assistance of legal aid and the solicitors' bill comes to £2,000. That £2,000 will have to be paid to the Legal Aid Board out of the damages unless it can be recovered from the other side in addition to the damages. However if he had to pay a contribution of £50 per month over ten months that would be taken into account and deducted from the amount that would be deducted from his damages.

Solicitors when consulted by a client who is seeking legal aid sometimes charge for the time preparing the legal aid application. Legal aid is not granted retrospectively so that amount cannot be reclaimed from the legal aid fund, though it will form part of the costs recoverable from the other side if the action is won. Many solicitors waive this charge unless completing the application is very complex and time-consuming.

It is quite a common tactic in litigation for one side or his solicitors to write to the Legal Aid Board complaining that the other side should not have been awarded legal aid. Sometimes it is because of a contention that that party's case is too weak to justify legal aid, sometimes it is on the basis that he has misled the Board about the state of his finances. Neighbour disputes often involve each side keeping an eye on the other in the hope of establishing new found wealth which might disqualify them from legal aid! In fact the Board very rarely responds favourably to such representations: it simply does not have the resources to consider them properly and hence tends to disregard them.

The normal rule in a case where the claim exceeds £1,000 is that the loser has to pay the winner's legal costs. However if the person who loses has legal aid that will not normally be applied. In deciding whether or not to make any costs order the court has to decide what is reasonable in the light of the legally aided loser's conduct in relation to the case and his resources[8]. The award made then might be restricted to the amount the loser had been adjudged capable of paying by way of contribution to his own legal aid. This protection from having to pay the other side's costs can be a reason why a party who feels able to handle his own case without a solicitor is better off being legally aided.

Legal aid normally covers being fully represented in respect of a case. An application for such legal aid takes several weeks to process. However in a suitable case it will be granted on an "emergency" basis. This can even by be done over the telephone or by fax if there is a need to make an immediate application. In domestic violence cases, for instance, the majority of legal aid applications are granted in this way.

There is also a scheme that enables a solicitor to give advice and assistance on a provisional basis without a decision on the matter's suitability for full legal aid being considered by the Legal Aid Board. The *Green Form* Scheme[9] enables advice to be given on this basis and representation for at least a short hearing can be given under the *Assistance by Way of Representation* (*ABWOR*) scheme. Advice is available without contribution to anyone whose income after allowances is less than £72 per week. The same principles about contribution and recoupment out of property recovered and preserved apply to ABWOR as do to full civil legal aid. The amounts of income on which eligibility and contribution are assessed are slightly different.

Certain solicitors have been granted *franchises* by the Legal Aid Board to administer legal aid. A firm having a franchise will be able to obtain legal aid more quickly, but it is a factor unlikely to make any difference to the nature of the advice or representation provided. The Green Paper discussed above has proposed eventually restricting legal aid work to franchisee firms.

---

[8] s12 Legal Aid Act 1988
[9] So named of course because the application form is green. This name has now been institutionalised by heading the form "Green Form"!

"No win: no fee" arrangements

Very recently Parliament has given approval to proposals enabling lawyers to take on certain types of cases on a "no win: no fee" basis[10]. Such arrangements, known as *conditional fees*, were previously illegal. They are likely to be most frequently used in personal injury cases, where a prospective plaintiff not eligible for legal aid, would have no other way of being able to fund the action. They may also be used in certain insolvency matters. In exchange for taking cases on such a basis solicitors and barristers will be able to charge up to double their normal rates. The Law Society has proposed an agreement solicitors would enter into with clients instructing them on this basis that would put a ceiling on the proportion of the damages recovered that the uplift can amount to at 25%. American style *contingency fees* where the lawyers take a proportion of the damages are not allowed. The litigant is still personally liable for out of pocket expenses, such as the cost of expert witnesses and court fees.

Even where such an arrangement is entered into, the person bringing the action could be liable for the other side's legal fees if he loses. Insurance for a relatively small premium will be available to protect against this possibility.

A word of warning

Litigants do tend to become obsessed with their litigation. Those conducting it themselves particularly find that it overtakes their lives. Litigation can be interesting but people not involved in it do not want to hear about it in detail. A lawyer who spent dinner parties discussing the minutiae of his cases would find invitations drying up very quickly. Lawyers usually have the advantage over litigants in such conversations about court cases in that they can be objective. There is nothing more tedious for the listener than to have to bear the brunt of a person going on about how someone else has wronged him. Sympathy for the wrong is rarely the result, more common is pity at what the wrong has reduced a previously interesting person to. In short, however strongly someone

---

[10] The Conditional Fee Agreements Order 1995

may feel about his case he should be aware of the danger of becoming a litigation bore and avoid it all costs!

Another and rather remoter danger is that of being declared a *vexatious litigant*. A person who abuses the court system by regularly commencing hopeless actions, may on the application of the attorney-general be declared a vexatious litigant. Once he has acquired that status he cannot then commence any civil action without first obtaining the leave of a High Court judge. Such orders though are made very infrequently[11] and it would take the commencing of several such actions before that step was taken against anyone.

---

[11] There have been less than thirty this century.

3. THE LEGAL PROFESSION

Solicitors and barristers

Most lawyers are solicitors, about 10% are barristers. Traditionally solicitors have been regarded as the person having a general all round knowledge to whom one takes a problem initially, and barristers were the specialist to whom the solicitor would refer particularly knotty problems, especially those where a lengthy court appearance was likely to be necessary. Often nowadays the position is reversed. Solicitors, particularly in big firms, may specialise in one area of law, whilst barristers will hold themselves out as being able to do any kind of case. Some will claim to be able to do every type of civil work, a few even combine that claim with a willingness to appear in the criminal courts.

Barristers often describe themselves as doing *common law* or *chancery* work. The significance of this distinction is gradually being eroded but it is still reflected in the fact that the two main divisions of the High Court are similarly divided: the *Queen's Bench Division* deals with common law matters, and there is a *Chancery Division*. The Law Reports are also divided into Queen's Bench and Chancery sections. For some reason this distinction has never really caught on amongst solicitors. Common law work tends to involve the more straight forward sort of case such as accidents causing injuries, breach of contracts and defamation. All the examples that are followed through this book would come into that category. Chancery work was originally concerned with trusts and the ownership of lands. Whilst for many chancery barristers badly drafted wills are a staple source of income, taxation and intellectual property rights, such as copyrights and trade marks, have become more abundant sources of work. Barristers are often known as *counsel* but never "a counsel" or "the counsel". A barrister asked by a receptionist who he works for may well reply "of counsel".

In theory at least a barrister is not able to turn down work because he does not approve of a prospective client's case. This principle is known as the "*cab-rank*" rule. It is eminently sensible. Everybody should be entitled to be represented. If that person's case is odious it is for the court to judge and treat it accordingly. Barristers should not want or have the power to judge cases, they merely present them. However once a person has told a barrister (or a solicitor) that the basis of his case is not in fact true, that lawyer cannot continue to represent him, unless he agrees to tell the court what he has told the lawyer. This happens most often in criminal cases when the defendant says something like, "I did it, but will you get me off anyway?".

The first, though not the second of these two rules is often disregarded. There are many chambers whose members more or less openly state that they never represent landlords against tenants or employers against employees. A barrister is entitled to refuse to accept a case if he is not to be paid a "proper professional fee". For these purposes legal aid rates are to be regarded as such a fee, so again in theory at least, a barrister cannot turn down work because it is legally aided. No such constraint applies to solicitors.

Solicitors have recently acquired rights of audience in all the civil courts. This right is though restricted to those, often former barristers, who have undergone training in advocacy. In practice most solicitors prefer to instruct barristers for lengthy or complex work. Laypeople are not normally entitled to instruct a barrister except through a solicitor[12]. Solicitors when they instruct a barrister usually talk of *briefing* him. To many it seems an unnecessary expense to use and pay two lawyers, particularly as the solicitor is likely to sit through the trial doing little more than taking a note. Partial justification for the system may come from the fact that because barristers do not deal directly with the public, they need far fewer support staff and other facilities and consequently have lower overheads. Typically a barristers' *chambers* (the word "office" is frowned upon) with twenty members might employ five administrative staff. A firm of twenty solicitors would employ at least fifteen, often a lot more. Consequently a barrister's fees on an hourly rate, although far from modest, tend to be less than a solicitor of equivalent experience and expertise would charge for doing the same work. For this reason solicitors often use barristers, particularly junior ones, to do work they could adequately handle themselves.

Every year between thirty and eighty barristers are appointed Q.C.'s: *Queen's Counsel*, a process also known as *taking silk*. They will then

---

[12] The exceptions enable certain professionals, such as accountants and surveyors, to seek a barrister's opinion directly on non-contentious matters.

restrict their practices to the highest paid and most demanding work. Many become judges, particularly those who after appointment as Q.C.'s do not have much success in attracting this type of work.

Lawyers' assistants

As well as passing on work to barristers, solicitors often employ "unqualified" assistants. Amongst these are *legal executives*. These are members of a professional body and have to pass examinations in law as well as gaining years of practical experience before being entitled to this title. Most of them work virtually unsupervised. There is no reason why a qualified legal executive should not provide as satisfactory service as a solicitor. They are not allowed however to practice on their own or become partners in solicitors' firms. Many solicitors' employees are referred to as *managing clerks*. This is an old fashioned term, which was used to describe an experienced clerk who was capable of doing much of the same work as a solicitor. The growth of legal executives has rather reduced the use of this description: there was never any formal recognition for it. Someone who has been working as a clerk all his life should be capable of doing most of the routine work involved in litigation, so long as he leaves the trickier to someone more qualified. It is fair to say that most experienced managing clerks are quite happy to refer matters to a solicitor or instruct a barrister when they get difficult. One would be advised to be wary of any nineteen year old held out by his employer to be a "managing clerk". Although the description is not strictly speaking wrong, so intangible is the job, it is a little misleading. Terms like *clerk*, *legal assistant* and *para-legal* are also used to describe unqualified people working in a solicitors' office.

Articled clerks were ones who had passed their solicitors' exams but were doing the two years necessary practical work before they could qualify. This quaint term was recently replaced by the more logical *trainee solicitor*. Trainees are often quite good at dealing with difficult points of law: their main task may well be legal research, but inevitably tend not to have so much knowledge of the practical aspects of the job.

Obviously the more qualified and experienced the person doing the work, the higher that person's charging rate will be. On the other hand an experienced solicitor should be able to work a lot faster than a trainee, who may need to keep checking things. It may well be that even if the solicitor's hourly rate is double the trainee's the actual amount charged for doing the same work is not much greater.

Barristers' chambers employ a *clerk* who is in charge of the administration. More progressive chambers may refer to him as a "practice manager" or "administrator". He is regarded by many as an awesome figure with the power to make or break a barrister's practice. Even if this is something of an exaggeration, his ability to allocate briefs sent to chambers gives him a standing that most administrative employees do not have. Traditionally he has been paid commensurately: 10% of the chambers' total income. As chambers can have up to fifty members this means he could have earned five times more than the average barrister! Few chambers are prepared to pay such amounts these days. Many clerks are on salaries- usually still substantial- or lower percentages.

Trainee barristers are known as *pupils*. Pupillage lasts a year, but during the second six months barristers are able to practise on their own. Pupils are expected to provide assistance to and go to court with members of their chambers, particularly the one who is allocated as their *pupil-master*[13]. Pupils are not paid, though many chambers do offer "scholarships" which typically will be a little more than a student grant.

Solicitors' and barristers' organisation and fees

Solicitors practice either alone or in partnership. They are not permitted to form limited companies, but they can employ other solicitors as well as unqualified staff. Barristers, although they share *chambers* and pool expenses, cannot even form partnerships. A barrister's fees, unlike a solicitor's invariably go straight into his own pocket. Barristers cannot however sue either the solicitor who instructs them or the lay client for their fees. The solicitor can be disciplined by the Law Society for failing to pay a barrister's fees, even if he has not received the money to do so from the lay client. Consequently almost all solicitors will insist on

---

[13] There is little consensus amongst women barristers about whether the use of the term "*pupil-mistress*" is desirable!

receiving the barrister's fees from their clients before sending any instructions to him. Barristers will not normally negotiate directly with lay clients about their fees. Such matters should be handled through the solicitor.

The calculation of solicitors' own fees can be something of mystery. Most are reluctant to commit themselves to doing any particular piece of contentious work for a fixed price. This is not unreasonable: it is often impossible to know how long something will take. However they should be willing to state what their hourly rate is.

Many solicitors bill by calculating an hourly rate and then adding a percentage *uplift* sometimes described as being for *care and conduct*. The more difficult the case the higher this uplift is likely to be. The justification for it is that solicitors spend a lot of time reflecting about their cases even when they are not actually engaged on them: "thinking in the bath" allowance it is sometimes described as. If a bill is presented at the end of a case where no fee level has been agreed, the adding of this uplift is normal and proper. On the other hand for a solicitor to agree an hourly rate and then attempt to charge an uplift on top of it is clearly wrong.

VAT is usually payable on the amount charged for legal fees. The solicitor should also be asked to confirm what the position in respect of this is when agreeing fees: very rarely will this be included in the initial quote.

Rights of audience

Only those with a *right of audience* are entitled to appear in courts. Litigants in person are always entitled to conduct their own cases. However limited companies do not have the same *legal personality* as their directors, which means that a director or other officer of a company does not have the automatic right to appear for it in court. Companies should only appear through a solicitor or a barrister. This rule may be relaxed in the county court, particularly in respect of small claims (see page 19). In the High Court it is more rigorously upheld, and an exception would only be made in respect of a company whose resources were such that it could not afford to pay lawyers to defend a claim made against it[14].

Barristers have a right of audience in every court. Solicitors do not have a general right to appear in "open court" in the High Court and Crown Court. However under the provisions of the courts and Legal Services Act 1990 they can apply to became *solicitor-advocates* whereupon they acquire such rights. All solicitors can appear in *chambers* matters in the High Court as well as having complete rights of audience in the county court and magistrates' courts. In practice- particularly in London- solicitors tend to prefer to instruct a barrister to appear in long or difficult hearings in the county court.

In *chambers* matters, people employed by solicitors as well as the solicitors themselves can appear. Legal executive have rights of audience in certain uncontested applications in the county courts. *Lay representatives* can appear on behalf of a litigant who is physically present at a small claims hearing[15]. Workers from organisations such as Citizens' Advice Bureaux may be willing to take on this task.

For cases where lay representatives are not able to appear, the alternative might be to have a *McKenzie*[16] friend. This is a person who attends court with a litigant to advise, suggest questions the litigant might ask of witnesses and provide moral support. Such a person does not have the right to address the court directly.

Complaints about solicitors and barristers

Complaints about solicitors can be made to the Solicitors Complaints Bureau (8 Domer Place, Leamington Spa, Warwickshire CV32 5AE, tel: 01926 820082). A report by the National Consumer Council in December 1994 made findings about that body which would have come as little surprise to anyone in the profession. In essence it provides a completely unsatisfactory means of making a complaint. It attempts to make any complainant reach some conciliation with the solicitor

---

[14] *Charles P Kinnell & Co v Harding Wace & Co* [1918] 1 KB 405

[15] CCR Ord 19

[16] After *McKenzie v McKenzie* [1971] where such a person was allowed to act by the court. The term has survived despite disapproval of the Court of Appeal in *R V Leicester City Justices, ex parte Barrow* [1991] 3 WLR 368.

complained of. Many complainants faced with this exhortation, simply don't bother to pursue the matter. This finds it way into the Bureau's statistics as a success! Although the public often see the Kafkaesque approach as a sign that the Bureau, which is funded by solicitors, is only interested in protecting the profession. In fact solicitors complained about suffer just as much from its inefficiencies as do complainers. To have a complaint that is not properly investigated, however unfounded or frivolous, hanging over one is time consuming and embarrassing. It is pressure from solicitors that may well lead to it being replaced by a more efficient and rational body.

Complaints about barristers can be made to the General Council of the Bar (3 Bedford Row, London WC1R 4DP, tel: 0171 242 0082). These are generally investigated rather more effectively than are complaints about solicitors.

Judges

The type of judge whom the county court litigant is most likely to come into contact with is a *district judge*. Until 1991 these were known as *registrars*. They were normally practising solicitors before their appointment. They deal with most of the preliminary applications that are heard in the county court and sit as the trial judge on claims up to £5,000. Claims over £5,000 are dealt with by *circuit judges*. These can have formerly been either barristers or solicitors, though until recently almost all appointments were from amongst barristers. It is almost a truism to say that ethnic minorities and women are badly under-represented amongst these and all classes of the judiciary. Circuit judges deal with trials where over £5,000 is claimed and most claims for possession of property or injunctions. The exact distribution of business between the two classes of judge varies from county court to court.

In the High Court in London the functions of district judges are carried out by *masters*. Away from London the High Court has *district registries*, usually in the same buildings as the county court[17], and the "lower grade" judicial work is done by district judges. High Court

---

[17] The use of the upper case for "High Court" and lower for "county court" is not as many readers might presume a typesetting error but the reflection of an historical anomaly!

judges, correctly known as *puisne judges*, are considerably higher up the judicial scale. They are automatically given a knighthood on appointment. They of course sit in the High Court and often make up the numbers in the Court of Appeal, whose permanent judges- *Lord Justices*[18]- are appointed from amongst the ranks of High Court judges. The *Lord Chief Justice* is in charge of the Criminal Division of the Court of Appeal and the *Master of the Rolls*, the Civil Division. At the top of the judicial pyramid are the *Lords of Appeal in Ordinary*, or the *"Law Lords"*. They make up the Judicial Committee of the House of Lords, and hear the small proportion of cases which they or the Court of Appeal deem suitable for further appeal after that court has made a ruling. The *Lord Chancellor*, a political appointee and the nearest there is in Britain to a "minister for justice" can and frequently does sit as a Law Lord.

At the other end of the scale there are chairmen of tribunals, the most numerous of which are industrial tribunals and social security tribunals.

At all levels of the judiciary much of the work is done by deputy judges. These are part time judges who can be either retired judges or (except in the Court of Appeal and House of Lords) practising lawyers. Deputy circuit judges are known as *recorders* except for those who have done it for less than three years who are only *assistant recorders*.

---

[18] These, unlike the judges of the House of Lords, are not Lords in the normal sense and do not sit in the parliamentary House of Lords.

4. LIMITATION PERIODS AND DELAY

An action has to be commenced within a certain period of the matter being complained of occurring. A failure to commence an action within a limitation period is probably the commonest cause of negligence actions against solicitors. Some solicitors lamentably regard the limitation date as the one on which they should start the action. However in normal circumstances such delay is deplorable in itself. In all but the most complicated claims proceedings should be commenced within six months of the solicitor being instructed. That should be ample time to obtain legal aid, if appropriate, a barrister's opinion if it is needed, conduct any enquiries and give the proposed defendant an opportunity to offer a settlement. If a solicitor takes any longer than this, his client is perfectly entitled to ask why. A frequent and perfectly proper reply will be that the solicitor is not prepared to commence proceedings until given sufficient funds to cover the costs of doing this!

The limitation periods for most claims is six years from the date the cause of action accrued[19]. However if damages for personal injuries[20] or defamation[21] are claimed this period is reduced to three years.

A limitation period does not run against a person until he is eighteen[22]. Therefore if a child is injured, even at birth, he will be able to sue in respect of those injuries at any time until he is twenty-one.

The cause of action accrues at the time the defendant does the act complained of. Often however no damage will be apparent for some time after he has done this. In that case an action can be brought for three years after the damage became apparent[23]. This exception is however subject to a "long-stop" provision preventing actions more than fifteen years after the act. It is most frequently relied upon in professional negligence cases. If, for instance an architect negligently designs a building, the defects may not show up for more than six years.

---

[19] ss2, 5 Limitation Act 1980
[20] s11 Limitation Act 1980
[21] s4A Limitation Act 1980
[22] s28 Limitation Act 1980
[23] s14A Limitation Act 1980

There is a similar exemption in personal injury cases where the damage caused does not manifest itself for some time[24]. This has been relied upon in asbestosis cases. It is not subject to any "long-stop" provision. If the three year period is missed in a personal injury claim, the court does have a discretion to allow the action to be commenced out of time[25].

Certain actions relating to trusts and special deeds attract a twelve year limitation period. The most important practical aspect of this is the fact that possession of land cannot be recovered more than twelve years after it was first occupied by a squatter[26].

Once an action is commenced delay can result in it being struck out. The most significant instance of this if a trial date has not been requested in a county court action within fifteen months of the *close of pleadings*[27]. There is also a general power to strike an action out for *want of prosecution*. This is normally only done after the court has made an "*unless order*" stating the action will be struck out if it is not proceeded with within a specified time[28].

---

[24] s11 Limitation Act 1980
[25] s33 Limitation Act 1980
[26] s15 Limitation Act 1980
[27] See page 49 for an explanation of when this occurs.
[28] CCR Ord 13 r2

5. COMMENCING AN ACTION

The county court summons

An action in the county court is started by filling in a form. For most types of action this will be headed "County Court Summons". Blank forms are available without charge from county court offices. Some can be prevailed to post these out, it will be necessary to collect them from others. At the same time ask for a list of current fees[29].

When completing this form the Plaintiff will first have to specify his own name and address. The section underneath that asks for the, "Address for service (and payment)" should be left blank unless a solicitor is acting. Then comes the space for the address of the defendant. This can be his residence or business. If the defendant is a company then it can be anywhere that the company carries on business or its registered office. The registered office should be stated on the company's letterheads. With small companies this is often the address of its accountants rather than anywhere owned by the company itself. If the registered office is known it is usually best to use that as the company's address. The next section asks for a brief description of the type of claim. This should be restricted to a few words such as, "Damages for injuries suffered in a road accident", "Compensation for shoddy goods", "Payment of an unpaid bill for plumbing work".

The particulars of claim

The most complex part of the summons is the section, "Particulars of the Plaintiff's Claim". For a small claim there is a lot to be said for merely writing as one might in a letter to a friend an account of what happened. However it is worth noting what is said on page 90 about awards of interest and putting words to the effect that, "Interest is claimed as

---

[29] Those payable at the time of writing are set out on pages 93 to 94 but they are frequently altered.

allowed for by s69 of the County Courts Act 1984". If no such claim is made at this stage, interest may not be added to the eventual damages. Avoid legalese and over formality, though on the other hand avoid being too forthright. The court will certainly not appreciate any views a plaintiff may want to express on his adversary's parentage!

Mrs Green (the facts of whose claim are set out on page 9) might write as follows:

> **Dear Sir,**
> **I wish to claim my money back and compensation for damage caused by a washing machine I bought from the Defendant's shop on 1 October 1995 for £450. I started using it the next day. It was satisfactory on the first few occasions I used it. However on October 11 it overheated and scorched the clothes that were in it. Smoke came out of the back and I had to call the fire brigade. The chief fireman said he had seen other washing machines like mine do this and that I should not use it again. My friend, Jennifer Watkins, was there when this happened and she will give evidence for me. I contacted the Defendant but he said what happens after goods leave the shop isn't his responsibility and that he won't do anything to help me.**
> **The value of the clothes in the washing machine was about £200 and I would like the cost of this. The smoke also damaged a section of my kitchen wall which will cost £50 to redecorate. I already have an estimate from Mr Reg Hollins who normally does our decorating. This is a total of £700. As well as this I would like to claim interest pursuant to s69 of the County Courts Act 1984 on this sum.**

For those who want to do things "properly", and to some extent this is expected by the courts in claims over the small claims limit, the following rules should be followed. It must be said that a great number of solicitors and a few barristers have difficulty sticking to them. The most fundamental rule is to only plead the facts that need to be proved to make out the case: not the evidence that is to be relied upon in support of them. This can be particularly difficult. However comparing the more formal pleading set out below with Mrs Green's letter will provide a relatively simple example of what should and should not be included.

The pleading should be set out in numbered paragraphs. In so far as possible each paragraph should deal with one allegation. It should conclude with an indented paragraph summarising the remedy claimed. This is known as *the prayer*.

Mrs Green's particulars of claim done formally might read as follows:

1. The Defendant is in the business of selling electrical equipment to the public.

2. On 1 October 1995 the Plaintiff bought a washing machine ("the Washing Machine") from the Defendant for £450.

3. There were by reason of s14 of the Sale of Goods Act 1979 implied in the contract by which the Plaintiff bought the Washing Machine terms that it would be reasonably satisfactory and fit for its purpose.

4. In breach of those terms the Washing Machine was not reasonably satisfactory and was not fit for its purpose in that on 11 October 1995 whilst being used for the purpose of washing clothes it overheated and emitted smoke.

5. The Plaintiff on 12 October 1995 informed the Defendant of this and evinced an intention to reject the Washing Machine.

6. The Plaintiff has refused to accept the Washing Machine back.

7. By reason of the overheating and smoking of the Washing Machine the Plaintiff has suffered loss and damage:

PARTICULARS

(i) The cost of replacing the clothes in the Washing Machine at the relevant time and which were irreparably damaged:

£200

(ii) The cost of redecorating a wall damaged by the smoke emitted from the washing machine:

£50

8. The Plaintiff claims and is entitled to interest on all sums claimed herein pursuant to s69 of the County Courts Act 1984 as aforesaid.

The Plaintiff therefore claims:
    (i) The return of £450;
    (ii) Damages;
    (iii) Interest as previously stated.

[signed and dated]

Some lawyers drafting these particulars of claim might talk of "the said washing machine" (only after it had been referred to for the first time). In paragraph 7 the damage might have been caused "by reason of the matters aforesaid" and the last part of the prayer it might be "interest as aforesaid". These pompous expressions are unnecessary. Lawyers have however been trained to use them and for them are as easily recognisable and decipherable as the equivalent ordinary English usage. Sometimes laypeople try to use them in the hope that they will sound like lawyers. This is very rarely successful. Usually the result is an ungrammatical mess, and often one that makes no sense however generously one tries to construe it.

No reference is made in these particulars to the observations of the fireman nor to the presence of Ms Watkins nor to the fact that the cost of repair derives from an estimate prepared by Mr Hollins. To prove her case Mrs Green only has to establish the defect and the cost of the decoration. What these people saw and said is merely evidence to support what she has to prove and should strictly speaking not be referred to in the particulars. As has already been stated, the distinction is a difficult one. As a general rule if in doubt about something it should be put in.

The same principles with a few additions apply to pleading if there is a claim for damages after an accident. When this happens the plaintiff's claim will be based on an allegation that the accident was caused by the negligence of the defendant.

If the plaintiff is claiming damages for being hurt he must attach a doctor's report to his particulars of claim. He must also list his *special damages* that is his financial loss, such as wages lost whilst he had time off work in a *schedule of special damage*[30].

---

[30] A fuller explanation about types of damages is given on page 106.

An example of such a claim arising out of not very serious injuries might be Mr White's claim against Ms Fawn.

1. On 24th September 1995 the Plaintiff was walking across the road on the pedestrian crossing on Exeter Road in Northampton close to the junction with Durham Road when he was struck by a Ford Escort car being driven east along Exeter Road by the Defendant.

2. The accident was caused by the negligence of the Defendant.

PARTICULARS OF NEGLIGENCE

(i) Failing to accord precedence to the Plaintiff;

(ii) Driving at a speed that was unsafe in all the circumstances;

(iii) Failing to keep any or any proper look out;

(iv) Failing to stop, slow down swerve or otherwise manage his car so as to avoid striking the Plaintiff;

(v) Failing to stop before reaching the pedestrian crossing.

3. As a consequence of the accident the Plaintiff has suffered personal injury and loss and damage. The Plaintiff's injuries consisted primarily of a badly sprained wrist caused when he fell to the ground after being struck by the Defendant's car. A report prepared by Dr Foster is annexed to these Particulars and details the Plaintiff's injuries. Particulars of the Plaintiff's special damage appear in the Schedule hereto.

4. The Plaintiff claims and is entitled to interest on all sums claimed herein pursuant to s69 of the County Courts Act 1984 as aforesaid.

The Plaintiff therefore claims:

(i) Damages;

(ii) Interest as previously stated.

[signed and dated]

SCHEDULE OF SPECIAL DAMAGE

(i) As a consequence of the accident the Plaintiff had to take four days off his work as a self-employed bookkeeper, and lost earnings of £80 per day:

£320

(ii) The Plaintiff's trousers were torn and irreparably

damaged in the accident. The replacement cost will be:
£25

(iii) The Plaintiff has had to attend the outpatients clinic of his local hospital on two occasions. His fares in visiting the hospital have totalled:
£10

(iv) The Plaintiff was treated on one occasion by a physiotherapist to whom he paid:
£25

In the case of a simple claim for an unpaid debt, such as Ms Black's, the particulars can be equally simple, merely referring to the invoice:

The Plaintiff's claim is for £1,350 being the amount outstanding on invoice no. 12435 submitted by the Plaintiff to the Defendant on 2 November 1995 for plumbing work done for him by her, and for interest pursuant to s69 of the County Courts Act 1984 on that sum.

Issuing the proceedings

The Plaintiff then sends or takes to the court two copies of the form and particulars of claim along with the appropriate fee, keeping it hardly needs be said a copy of everything including the cheque for himself. The court should then *issue* the proceedings. There is a fair chance that some officious clerk will spot a defect in the form and return it to the would-be plaintiff. If that happens, merely correct it in the way the clerk insists it should be done, regardless of whether what he is saying actually seems to be right. If nothing is heard from the court after a fortnight, it is worth making enquiries about whether the forms nave been lost. Before doing that try to find out whether the payment cheque has been presented.

The defence

If all goes well, the defendant will be sent the summons and particulars of claim along with a form asking whether or not he admits the plaintiff's claim.

If he does not admit it he should send a *defence* to the court. This should set out why he objects to paying the money that the plaintiff has claimed. If appropriate, he may also make a *counterclaim*. The same principles apply to the drafting of these. It is necessary to respond to every allegation in the particulars of claim. Some of this will be "admitted", for instance in Mrs Green's case that there was a sale of a washing machine, some will be "denied", for instance the fact that the machine was defective. Other parts will be "not admitted". This means that the defendant is not in a position to say whether something claimed by the plaintiff is in fact true. In Mr White's claim, Ms Fawn is unlikely to know the extent of the injuries he has suffered, so she can neither admit them nor deny them. By *not admitting* she is requiring him to prove them.

Mr Blue might write if he relied on an informal defence:

> I do not accept what Mrs Green says except that I did sell her the washing machine on 1 October 1995 and the agreed price was £450, although only £225 of this has been paid. It came with a manual that said in no circumstances should it be filled with more than 5kg of clothes. I also expressly explained this to Mrs Green when she bought the machine. She came into my shop on 12 October claiming that it had "caught fire" and demanding that I give her money back and compensation. I asked her what clothes she had had in it at the time. She said four sheets. On further enquiry I established that two of these were for a double bed and two for a single bed. I should estimate that together they would weigh at least 10kg.
>
> It was because of this overloading that it has been damaged. I do not accept responsibility. Even if I were responsible I do not see how Mrs Green could be entitled to £200 for the sheets she claims were in there. At very most they would cost £80 to replace.
>
> The terms I agreed to sell Mrs Green the machine were that she pay me £225 immediately and the balance by a post-dated cheque also for £225, which should have been met on 1 November. She cancelled that cheque. I am still entitled

to the £225 and interest as specified by s69 of the County Courts Act 1984 on it.

A formal version of this in response to Mrs Green's own formal particulars of claim might read:

DEFENCE

1. It is admitted that the Defendant is in the business of selling electrical equipment to the public.
2. It is admitted that on 1 October 1995 the Defendant sold the Washing Machine to the Plaintiff.
3. The agreed price for the washing machine was £450.
4. The Plaintiff paid the agreed price by way of a cheque for £225 and a further cheque dated 1 November 1995 for £225.
5. It is admitted that the terms implied by s14 of the Sale of Goods Act 1979 applied to the sale of the washing machine.
6. It is not admitted that the washing machine broke down in the way described in paragraph 4 of the Particulars of Claim.
7. If the washing machine did break down in the way described, it did so because the Plaintiff had overloaded the machine in breach of the manufactures' instructions and the express warning given to her orally not to do so by the Defendant at the time she bought the machine.
8. Paragraphs 5 and 6 of the Particulars of Claim are admitted except that the Defendant maintains that the Plaintiff was not entitled to reject the Washing Machine and that he was entitled to refuse to accept it back.
9. It is denied that the Plaintiff has suffered the loss claimed or that she entitled to the damages or interest claimed.

COUNTERCLAIM

10. The Defendant repeats paragraphs 3 and 4 of the Defence.
11. The cheque dated 1 November 1995 has not been honoured by the Plaintiff's bankers because the Plaintiff has instructed them not do so.
12. The Defendant remains entitled to the sum of £225.

13. The Defendant is also entitled to and claims interest pursuant to s69 of the County Courts Act 1984.
The Defendant therefore claims:
    (i) The sum of £225;
    (ii) Interest thereon as stated.

Admitting the claim

If the defendant is prepared to admit the plaintiff's claim, he should not serve a defence but make the admission on the form sent to him by the court. He can also on that form ask for time to pay the debt. If he makes a sensible offer, it is likely that the court will approve it, and the plaintiff will gain little from trying to insist on earlier payment. If the defendant does not then pay as he has offered, the plaintiff can rely on the various methods of enforcement discussed in chapter 12.

Judgment in default of defence

If no defence or admission is served within 14 days of the summons being served upon the defendant, the plaintiff is entitled to enter a *default judgement*[31]. If the claim is for an ascertainable debt- rather than damages- (as in Ms Black's but not Mrs Green's or Mr White's claims), judgement may be entered for the final amount on the Plaintiff completing the form N225A, which should be available from the court. If the claim is for damages, the form to be completed is N234. There will then be a hearing for those damages to be assessed. The plaintiff will be sent a note by the court which tells him the date that service is deemed to have taken place. It is advisable to send in the request for judgement very shortly after the fourteen days have expired. If the defendant subsequently sends in a defence, he will be in a weaker position than if he does so without the judgement having been entered.

A judgement entered in default of defence can be set aside on the application of the defendant[32]. However the court will be reluctant to do

---

[31] CCR Ord 9 r6
[32] CCR Ord 37 r4

this unless the defendant can show there is a serious issue to be tried. He should swear an affidavit setting out what his defence is. (Affidavits are discussed on pages 47 to 48). The considerations the court will have regard to on such an application will be similar to those applied when it is the plaintiff who is seeking summary judgement (see pages 55 to 56). The defendant is likely to have to pay the costs of having the judgement set aside, though if the claim is under £1,000 the court may well make no order. However if the summons was not served upon him at all, perhaps because it was lost in the post, he will have an automatic right to set the judgement aside[33].

Choice of court

The plaintiff is entitled to commence an action in whichever county court he likes. If a defence is entered to a claim for a debt, it will automatically be transferred to the court for the area where the defendant lives or carries on business. Even if just damages are claimed, the court has a discretion to transfer it and the defendant can make an application for it to do so.

Actions of the sort discussed in this book could all be commenced in the Queen's Bench Division of the High Court by issuing a *writ*. A *statement of claim* which contains the same matters as the particulars of claim should be written (*endorsed*) on this writ. Service is normally effected by the plaintiff rather than the court. Commencing an action for a relatively small amount in the High Court has very little to recommend it, particularly for the litigant in person. The fees are higher, the procedure is more complex, the masters and judges are used to a more professional standard of presentation and have less patience for the inevitable errors of litigants in person.

---

[33] CCR Ord 37 r3

Further pleadings

A plaintiff has a right to serve a *reply* to the defendant's defence[34]. This is usually only done where there is also a counterclaim in which case the response will be a *reply and defence to counterclaim*.

Quite frequently one party will seek *further and better particulars* of the other's pleadings. This is a request for more information about what is stated in those pleadings. Lawyers, barristers particularly, have a great deal of fun with these requests. One asks the other side about an obscure detail of the pleading and the other counters with the response that the request is actually for evidence not for matters that are strictly pertinent to the pleading. Occasionally these requests are necessary so that each side knows where it stands in relation to the other's case. However usually they are overlooked when the matter comes to trial. Litigants have every right to be suspicious if their solicitors tell them such a request is being made: more often than not it will serve no purpose other than increasing the lawyers' fees.

A variation on and generally rather more valuable than further and better particulars are *interrogatories*. These are questions about the subject matter of the action served by one party to the action on another. They can be served on a party on two occasions without the court's leave and on further occasions if leave is applied for and granted. They should specify a period of time, at least 28 days, in which they are to be answered. The answer must be in the form of an affidavit. If a party on whom interrogatories are served objects to answering them, he has fourteen days in which to apply to the court for them to be set aside.

An example of an effective interrogatory might be if Mrs Green asking Mr Blue:

Have any other customers who bought washing machines complained to you about them in the last year?

A *notice to admit* is a notice requiring the other side to admit facts that, if it is served on the defendant, were either denied or not admitted in its defence. If served on the plaintiff, it can apply to any facts that

---

[34] Although the Woolf Report recommends that such a pleading should only be served with the leave of the court.

appear to be in dispute as a result of the particulars of claim.

If a notice to admit is served on a party who then refuses to admit the fact, and that fact is proved at trial, that party proving the fact will usually get his costs of doing so even if he loses on the main issue.

Mrs Green might serve a notice to admit on Mr Blue, requiring him to admit that the washing did break down and emitted smoke. That way she probably won't need to call the fireman as a witness. If Mr Blue doesn't admit it and the fireman has to come to court and there is a finding by the judge that the machine did do that, Mr Blue will have to pay the costs of bringing the fireman to court.

6. APPLICATIONS AND PROCEDURES BEFORE TRIAL

The form of application

In the course of an action it will often be necessary for a party to apply to the court for something: summary judgement, an interim payment, an attachment of earnings order. Applications made before judgement are known as *interlocutory applications*. Applications in the county court are made on forms. For some types of application there is a specific form, which will be identified in the text. For most however the application is in the following general form[35]. All of it should be written out leaving blanks for those parts that are to be completed by the court

In the [name of court] County Court

                                               [Court number]

Between

[Name of Plaintiff]   **Plaintiff**

                          and

[Name of Defendant]   **Defendant**

                    Notice of Application

I wish to apply for:
[e.g. *Summary judgement pursuant to CCR Order 9 rule 14 on the ground that there is no real defence to the claim which ground is more fully particularised in the affidavit herewith***]**

Signed [plaintiff's (or defendant's) (or either's solicitor's) name and address for service]

---

[35] Practice Form N244

[Date]

THIS SECTION TO BE COMPLETED BY THE COURT

TO the plaintiff/ defendant
TAKE NOTICE that this application will be heard by the district judge [or judge]

at   on   at o'clock

IF YOU DO NOT ATTEND THE COURT WILL MAKE SUCH ORDER AS IT THINKS FIT

In the High Court the normal method of applying to the court is by issuing a summons. This is best done on a *pro forma* that can be obtained from any law stationer.

Affidavits

At several points throughout this book the reader will be told that he requires an affidavit to support a certain application. An affidavit is a sworn statement of fact. It should be headed with the title of the action. It should then start with a statement giving the *deponent*'s (maker's) name, occupation and address, for instance:

> **I, Fred Joseph Bloggs, dustman, of 1 Acacia Avenue, London W1 make oath and say as follows:**

It should be bound as a book, preferably with green tape, though stapling along the side will usually be acceptable[36].

Often solicitors and their employees swear affidavits on behalf of their clients. In that case they must specify the capacity in which the affidavit is sworn and that they have authority to make it. The affidavit should

---

[36] CCR Ord 20 r10

contain a statement identifying the party on whose behalf it is sworn, particularly if it is sworn by someone, such as a solicitor, who is not a party.

If the affidavit refers to documents, copies of these should be *exhibited*. This is normally done by, immediately after the first reference to any document, saying:

> **"There is now produced and shown to me marked 'FJB1'[37] a bundle of documents. Page 1 of that bundle is..."**

The exhibits should be bound up in the same way as the affidavit.

The affidavit can be sworn in front of a solicitor, though irritatingly not the one who is acting for the person on whose behalf it is sworn. Other solicitors will witness its swearing for a nominal fee. It can also be sworn in front of the court staff without a fee. Whoever it is sworn in front of will endorse that they have witnessed the swearing of it and have seen the exhibits. Any alterations will have to be initialled. If the person making the affidavit does not wish to make a religious oath, he can affirm and the affidavit is then strictly speaking an *affirmation*.

It is hard to give general guidelines about the contents of the affidavit, except that it should of course be relevant to the application it supports. If something is said that is *hearsay* (see page 77), then the source of the information should be stated. It should be set out in numbered paragraphs and use ordinary English. Some solicitors use phrases like "verily believe"[38], "honourable court" and "humbly petition". These are pointless.

Directions in claims over £1,000

In most cases where over £1,000 is claimed *automatic directions* apply. The main types of actions where these rules do not apply are those arising out of consumer credit agreements[39] and where the action is to

---

[37] I.e. after Fred Joseph Bloggs.
[38] The authors of *Civil Litigation* (see the glossary) point out that if dictated this arcane phrase may be typed as an embarrassing "variably believe".
[39] CCR Ord 17 r11(d).

recover possession of land[40] or goods[41]. Claims between husband and wife whether based on matrimonial law principles or not are also excluded[42]. Otherwise actions which are for the recovery of money will be subject to the automatic directions. These require the parties to do a number of things without any specific instruction to do so from the court.

The starting point for the automatic directions timetable is the *close of pleadings*. This is 14 days after the defence has been served, unless the defence was accompanied by a counterclaim, in which case it is 28 days.

Discovery and inspection

The first stage in the automatic directions is *discovery*, which should take place within 28 days of the close of pleadings. This involves each party preparing a list of all the documents that it has that are relevant to the issues. Everything that is relevant has to be stated in this list even if it would be in that party's interest not to disclose them. The only exception is documents that have come into existence specifically for the purpose of assisting that party in connection with the dispute and any communications he may have had with his own solicitor: these are referred to as being *privileged*.

For instance in Mrs Green's case, suppose she had a receipt for the sheets she says were damaged in the machine and it showed that they were bought for a total of £24-99, she would still have to list it despite the fact that it would damage her claim that they were worth £200. On the other hand if she had obtained a report from an engineer telling her that the accident was her fault because she had overloaded the machine, she would not need to list that as it would be privileged.

A person representing himself could quite properly just write out a list of all the relevant documents. As well as ones still in his possession he should add on ones that he has had but no longer has. This would include the receipt if it had been lost. Strictly speaking in this part of the

---

[40] CCR Ord 17 r11(i)
[41] CCR Ord 17 r11(e)
[42] CCR Ord 17 r11(q)

list should be any relevant letters he has sent to anyone else: the originals of these will no longer be in his possession even though copies are likely to be. The list should conclude with a statement to the effect, "There are further documents in my possession but these are privileged." Solicitors preparing these lists do so on a *pro forma*[43] which is divided into three sections. The first section is for documents which are still in the party's possession, the second for those which are no longer in his possession and the third those which are privileged. If litigants in person can get hold of a copy of this form, they will find it easier to use than setting out all the documents in a letter.

The next stage after discovery and closely related to it is *inspection*, which should take place seven days later. This is where each side gets the opportunity to actually see the documents the other has listed on discovery. The easiest way to do that is by each sending the other photocopies of the documents. If vast numbers of documents have been disclosed it may be preferable, particularly from the point of view of a litigant in person who may not have free access to a photocopier, for there to be an inspection of originals. Strictly speaking this should be at the premises of the parties' or their solicitors'. If one party is represented by a solicitor and the other is not it would be sensible for the unrepresented one to take the documents to the solicitor's office in exchange for being allowed free use of the photocopier to enable him to copy the other sides' documents. If the exchange is done by posting photocopies it is normal for solicitors to charge at a rate of about 25p per page for this. In practice solicitors do not object to paying each other for this, knowing that they can in due course pass the charge onto their clients or the Legal Aid Board. After all if they objected to the other side's charges, someone might challenge their own! A litigant in person faced with a bill for photocopying at that rate could quite properly refuse to pay more than the 10p or so he has inserted into the machine at the public library, or he should levy a similar charge on the solicitors for the copying he has had to do to comply with his own obligations.

---

[43] Form N265 prepared by the Solicitors Law Stationery Society Ltd.

Witness statements

The next stage is the preparation and serving of *witness statements*, which has to be done within ten weeks of the close of pleadings. These statements are in some ways similar to the particulars of claim and defence that the parties will have prepared at the beginning of the action but are much wider ranging documents. The letter Mrs Green might have written when she was commencing the small claim (see page 35) could easily be adapted into a witness statement. Strictly speaking she should not have referred to what the fireman said to her as that is the evidence of someone else and coming from her it amounted to *hearsay*. As a general rule hearsay evidence is not admissible, a witness in his statement and in court should only state what he perceived himself, not what someone else has told him. (See page 77 for a more detailed explanation.)

Experts' reports

As well as statements of the witnesses who are going to say what actually happened, it may be necessary to find experts who can express an opinion about what happened. In an action, such as Mr White's, where someone has been injured a doctor's report is absolutely essential. Sometimes more than one doctor will be required: if a person has suffered a broken leg and damages to his eyes in an accident, different specialists will be needed to comment on each injury. In Mrs Green's case an engineer will be needed to express a view on why the machine over-heated. Possibly also the fireman could give evidence of his experience that this type of machine is prone to over-heating. However the courts are somewhat conservative in what they regard to be an expert and may be reluctant to accept that a fireman is an expert on washing machines!

The automatic directions provide for a limit of two expert witnesses per side[44]. In cases where damages are claimed for personal injuries, up to three are allowed, including two doctors and one other type of expert

---

[44] CCR Ord 17 r11(3)(b)(ii)

witness[45]. If there are good reasons for needing to have more experts, an application can be made to the court for permission to do this. An attempt should be made to reach agreement with the other side about the need for this, in which case the application to the court will be unnecessary.

Normally experts will prepare their own reports. However it is important to let them know exactly what it is they are supposed to be expressing an opinion on. Mrs Green might write to the engineer she has asked to inspect and report on her washing machine in the following terms:

> **I own a Yatsuka 220M washing machine serial number 1234567, which I new purchased from Blue Electrics on 1 October 1995. On 10 October 1995 the machine overheated, emitted smoke and scorched the clothes that were in it. The load in it at the relevant time consisted of two sheets and five blouses which weighed in total when dry about 7kg.**
>
> **Mr Blue in defending this claim has alleged that the machine would only over heat in this way because it was overloaded.**
>
> **I should be grateful if you would inspect the machine and prepare a report that may be used in court proceedings dealing with the following questions:**
>
> **(i) What caused the machine to overheat?**
>
> **(ii) Does the machine appear to have been overloaded at the time it overheated?**
>
> **(iii) Is it normal for washing machines to overheat because they are overloaded (regardless of whether or not you feel this one was)?**

Exchanging statements and reports

These statements- those of ordinary and expert witnesses- once prepared should be exchanged simultaneously. The normal procedure is for each side to promise the other not to open the other's until theirs are

---

[45] CCR Ord 17 r11(7)(a)

received. To achieve this the statements must be sent in a clearly marked envelope so there can be no danger of their being opened prematurely by mistake.

Setting down

The next stage is for the plaintiff to apply to the court to *set down* (list) the matter for trial. This can be done by letter which should state how long the trial will last and specifying dates on which the parties would not wish it to take place. A fee (£50 at the time of writing is payable at this stage). The letter should be addressed to the chief clerk of the court. Mrs Green might write as follows (assuming her claim is for more than £1,000, otherwise the procedure discussed on page 54 applies):

> **Dear Chief Clerk,**
> **Re Green v Blue: case no 123456**
> **This matter is now ready for trial. I estimate that it will last about three hours. The defendant's solicitor agrees with this time estimate. I should be grateful if it could be set down for the first available date. Could you please avoid 1-15 October as I shall be on holiday during that time.**
> **I enclose a cheque for £50.**
> **Yours faithfully**

This request for a hearing date should be made within six months of the close of pleadings[46]. It is absolutely crucial that it is done within fifteen months. If it is not the action is automatically *struck out*[47]. This means it is treated as dismissed. Only in the most exceptional circumstances will a plaintiff be able to get an action reinstated after it has been struck out for failure to comply with the fifteen months rule[48].

---

[46] CCR Ord 17 r11 3(d)
[47] CCR Ord 17 r11(9)
[48] See *Rastin v British Steel* [1994] 1 WLR 732

Dealing with a dilatory opponent

Time limits except for the draconian fifteen month rule are frequently ignored by solicitors. It would certainly be fair to say that no request is made to set down the majority of actions within the six month period.

If one's opponent is dragging his feet, then the best course is to first write a letter asking him to get a move on. If no response is received a firmer letter a week or so later should be sent. If that does not produce the desired result an application can be made to the court for an order debarring that party from proceeding with or defending the action. On hearing such an application the court will normally make an order that the defaulting party do something by a specified date and will in default be debarred from proceeding or defending: known as *an unless order*. If there is a good reason for the delay, perhaps it has not been possible to take a statement from a witness who is on a lengthy holiday, the court will often agree to extend the time without making such an order. On the other hand the fact that a party or his solicitor claims to be too busy to do things within the time limits will rarely be regarded as a good reason for delay.

Solicitors may sometimes try to intimidate litigants in person into accepting that delays are inevitable and giving the impression that it is only the naivety of a non-lawyer that could make anyone believe that time tables are meant to be complied with. There certainly are many solicitors who are happy to acquiesce in each others' delays but there is nothing commendable or professional about it. It is very rarely in a plaintiff's interests to hold matters up, more often than not is in the defendant's as well to speed along a case. Litigants in person (and similarly the clients of solicitors) should therefore pay scant regard to anything said by a solicitor about delays being normal or proper.

In cases to which the provision for automatic directions do not apply the court will usually order a directions hearing, sometimes known as a *pretrial review* where directions will be given. The directions given are normally to much the same effect as the automatic directions. However at a directions hearing the parties can ask for any special directions that appear appropriate to the case.

Directions in small claims

Where there is a small claim (currently one under £1,000 but likely to soon be raised to £3,000) many county courts automatically list the matter for a hearing after the defence has been served. This is obviously a sensible course but it is not universally followed nor does it ever apply where the claim is for a greater amount. Sometimes even in small claims the court will order a directions hearing known as a *pre-arbitration* hearing.

If there is not to be such a hearing the court should estimate the likely length of the trial before listing it. Each party will be directed to send to the other not less than 14 days before the hearing copies of the documents that are in their possession[49]. This effectively combines the discovery and inspection stages of an action for more than the small claims limit. Not less than 7 days before the hearing experts' reports have to be exchanged and each side must send to the other a list of the witnesses he intends calling.

Where a pre-arbitration hearing is ordered, it is likely that the district judge will give directions to the same effect as these, unless there is something in the case that makes special directions desirable.

Summary judgement

Some cases are so clear cut that they can be decided without a full trial. This is a procedure known as obtaining *summary judgement*. It is often referred to even in the county court as "*Order 14*", after the Rule of the Supreme Court that governs the application when it is made in the High Court. For some reason this is the one Order number that is familiar to virtually every lawyer. In the county court it is governed by Order 9 rule 14 and is only available for claims of more than £1,000. In neither court can it be used for claims for possession of land[50] or defamation, false imprisonment or malicious prosecution[51].

---

[49] CCR Ord 6 r3

[50] Although there is a similar procedure for evicting squatters: CCR Ord 24 rr1-7.

[51] CCR Ord 9 r14(1)(b),(c)

The decision whether or not to grant summary judgement is made by the court on a consideration of each side's case as set out in affidavits. As a general rule it is not a suitable procedure for deciding who is telling the truth as neither side will be able to test the evidence of the other by cross-examination. It is rarely used in accident cases. The basis on which the court approaches the application is by assuming that everything the defendant says is true unless it is quite obviously nonsense, and deciding whether on the assumption that it is true there is a defence.

Suppose in Mrs Green's claim, Mr Blue had put in a defence stating that he shouldn't be liable because any faults were down to the manufacturer not him. This is simply not right in law: a retailer is liable for defective goods he sold though he may well have a right of indemnity from the manufacturer. In that case summary judgement would be granted.

Sometimes where the district judge thinks that there is theoretically a defence but that it is extremely dubious- the term "shadowy" is often used- he may give *conditional leave to defend*. This means that judgement will be ordered in favour of the plaintiff unless the defendant pays into court some or all of the money claimed. This has the effect that if the plaintiff does eventually obtain judgement, there should be money available to satisfy it. While the action continues the money remains in court earning a reasonable amount of interest which, subject to any judgement in favour of the plaintiff, the defendant will get the benefit of. If the defendant can show that he is extremely poor and could not afford to pay the money in, he may avoid such an order[52]. This argument is more likely to be accepted from a legally aided person.

The application for summary judgement is made on the standard county court application form. It should be accompanied by an affidavit setting out the relevant circumstances. That affidavit must contain a statement to the effect that the maker of the affidavit believes there is no defence to the action[53]. The defendant can and should, if he contests the action, swear an affidavit in reply.

---

[52] *MV Yorke Motors v Edwards* [1982] 1 WLR 444
[53] CCR Ord 9 r14(2)

Striking out the action

The nearest equivalent to summary judgement in favour of the defendant is if he can persuade the court to strike out the claim of the plaintiff[54]. This procedure can be used to attack any pleading in an action and is occasionally used by a plaintiff to strike out a defence in circumstances where he cannot obtain summary judgement. The simplest basis for striking out particulars of claim and hence the whole action is that they show no cause of action. When the mother of one of the Yorkshire Ripper's victims sued the Police for their alleged negligence in failing to capture him before he killed her daughter the claim was struck out on this basis[55]. However negligent the Police may have been, they were not in breach of any duty to the victim or her mother which could have given her a claim against them. A very weak action can also be struck out on the basis that it is "scandalous, frivolous or vexatious". There is a more general power to strike out actions and pleadings that are "an abuse of the process of the court". This is most frequently applied where the action in effect seeks to overturn a decision already made by another court. A person who had pleaded guilty to wounding and had been sent to prison had his claim for negligence against the solicitors who had advised him in that case struck out on this basis[56].

The procedure again involves the use of the standard application form. An affidavit is necessary unless the only ground for striking it out is that the pleading discloses no cause of action. Sometimes where the court is inclined to strike out an action the court will allow the defective pleading to be amended so that it does amount to a sustainable claim. Where this happens the plaintiff can expect to be ordered to pay the costs wasted by his failure to get it right in the first place.

Interim payments

As cases often take quite a long time to reach court, there is a procedure

---

[54] CCR Ord 13 r5
[55] *Hill v Chief Constable of West Yorkshire* [1989] AC 53
[56] *Somasundram v M Julius Melchoir & Co* [1988] 1 WLR 1394

which enables a plaintiff to apply to the court for an award of damages pending trial[57]. In the county court it is only available where the main claim is over £1,000.

An order for such a payment will only be made where the court is convinced that the person making the application has a strong case. Where the claimant is an individual who does not appear to be particularly wealthy, the courts may be reluctant to make an award in any but the most overwhelming cases. If he does not win at trial he will be under an obligation to repay the money, but may well have spent it all, making it difficult for the defendant to ever get it back.

In personal injury cases an interim payment won't even be considered unless the defendant is a public authority or a wealthy person or company or is insured in respect of the claim[58].

If the person making the claim needs the money for a purpose particularly associated with the accident the courts might be more sympathetic to the application. An example of this would be an accident victim who required special private medical treatment which he could not afford. The fact that there is no specific need for it is not though a bar to its recovery.

In debt cases where part but not all of the debt is admitted, the court might well make an order for the interim payment of that part of the debt which is admitted. Similarly if a landlord is claiming possession of a property and rent arrears, there may well be an interim order for the payment of the rent arrears pending the trial on the question of possession. If the tenant appears to have a sustainable counterclaim, such an order is much less likely.

An application for an interim payment is made by filling in the standard application form. This should be accompanied by an affidavit. That should state the reasons why the plaintiff believes he has a strong case. It should detail any special need he has for the interim payment. If a payment into court or a without prejudice offer has been made this, in reverse of the usual rule about keeping such matters secret from the judge, may be disclosed in the affidavit[59].

---

[57] CCR Ord 13 r12, which incorporates RSC Order 29 Part II (the similar High Court provision) into the county court

[58] RSC Ord 29 rule 11(2)

[59] *Fryer v London Transport Executive* (1982) *The Times* 4 December

Security for costs

A person being sued on tenuous grounds may fear that he is likely to incur considerable legal costs which he may have no means of recovering against the plaintiff. In some circumstances the court will require the plaintiff to pay the likely amount of the defendant's costs into court as a condition of his being allowed to continue the action. The mere fact that the plaintiff is poor and that his cases seems weak will not be sufficient grounds for doing this[60]. If he lives abroad, which for this purpose means outside England or Wales, such an order may be made. Similarly it may be made against a plaintiff who has misstated his address when commencing the action, a plaintiff who is merely a nominal plaintiff and an impecunious limited company.

The court does not have to make an order merely because the defendant fits into one of those categories. It will consider the strength of the claim, the conduct of the defendant and, in the case of a foreign plaintiff, whether he has assets in England or Wales.

Theoretically a litigant in person can make an application for security for costs. This would normally be restricted to the costs that he was likely to recover if they were assessed on the litigant in person basis[61]. However it might also be possible to seek them on the basis of what they would be if he were to instruct a solicitor. This line might well find sympathy with the court if the defendant could show that he would face financial ruin if he incurred a solicitors' bill, which he could not recover from the plaintiff.

The application for security can be made at any stage of the action: the earlier the better generally from the defendant's point of view. The application should be supported by an affidavit setting out the basis on which an order may be made against that plaintiff and any particular reason why it is appropriate to do so.

---

[60] RSC Ord 23, which is applied in the county court as well as the High Court.
[61] See page 94.

Interlocutory Appeals

If a decision on an interlocutory matter is made by a district judge it is usually possible to appeal from his decision to a circuit judge. The circuit judge has a considerably wider discretion in considering such an appeal than the Court of Appeal does when considering an appeal against a final order[62]. The circuit judge can substitute his own discretion for the district judge's.

However, just as with final appeals, a litigant in person would not be well advised to make such an appeal without seeking legal advice: the district judge will have been able to take a view of the merits of his position that is more informed and objective than the litigant's.

The appeal must be made within five working days of the original decision[63], though the circuit judge does have a discretion to extend that period. A fee is payable. The standard county court application form can be used. If the appeal is made late, as well as seeking to overturn the district judge's decision leave should be sought on the form to appeal out of time.

Payment into court

Once proceedings are issued a defendant can sometimes protect his position by making a payment into court. This should be done where he believes that the plaintiff has a reasonable chance of succeeding but will not recover all the damages he is claiming.

Once a payment in is made the plaintiff normally has 21 days to decide whether to accept it. If he does so, he can ask the court to give him that money and the action will be at end. If the claim is for over £1,000, he will be entitled to his legal costs in addition. If he does not accept it, then there is a risk that he will have to pay all the Defendant's costs after the twenty-one days have expired even if he wins at trial. Only if he "beats" the payment in by obtaining more damages will he get his legal costs incurred after that date. In addition he is likely to be ordered to pay those the defendant has incurred after that date.

---

[62] See page 91
[63] CCR Ord 13 r1

To give a very simple example: suppose in Mr White's road accident there had been payment in on 1 November 1995 of £1,500. By that date Mr White had incurred £400 worth of recoverable costs. If he takes the £1,500 he will also be entitled to that £400.

However suppose he rejects it and the matter proceeds to a trial. Ms Fawn's insurer's keep up their contention that the accident was entirely his fault. The judge does not agree with that and finds Ms Fawn was completely to blame. However he only awards Mr White £1,300 damages. The recoverable costs incurred after the payment in might be around £800 for each side. Mr White would receive the £1,300 plus the £400 earlier costs, but not the £800 he incurred after the payment in. Out of that £1,700 the insurers would be entitled to deduct the £800 later costs reducing the payment to £900. Mr White would have to pay his own solicitors at least £1,200, probably more as a litigant's own solicitor is usually entitled to charge him more than will be recovered from the other side. Mr White despite having won his case will actually be out of pocket!

7. THE HIGH COURT

The vast majority of litigation is commenced in the county court and except where there is a good reason for doing otherwise, reference in this book to court procedure has been to the county court procedure. Until 1991 a claim for more than £5,000 had to be commenced in the High Court[64], though most actions which were for less than around £25,000 were transferred at an early stage to the county court. Now there is no limit on the amount of damages that can be claimed in the county court. Virtually any claim can be brought in the High Court, although there are costs penalties for starting an action in the High Court that was more suitable to the county court[65]. The most significant exception to this are actions for personal injuries which unless the amount claimed exceeds £50,000, must be brought in the county court[66]. The few actions which have to be brought in the High Court include defamation claims, proceedings in connection with a trust worth over £30,000, judicial review[67], and certain injunctions[68].

The High Court is divided into three main divisions: the Queen's Bench, Chancery and Family. The type of work each deals with is discussed in relation to barristers (on page 24). Within these Divisions there are a number of sub-Divisions. The *Official Referees* sit as judges in both Divisions, They deal with factually complicated cases, typically involving building or computer disputes. There is a *Commercial Court* within the Queen's Bench Division. This tends to deal with shipping contracts, insurance and reinsurance, international banking agreements and similar matters[69]. The Commercial Court is regarded as more efficient than the rest of the High Court and as a result there are more actions commenced in it than it can cope with. Many are transferred, usually to the Queen's Bench Division. Within the Chancery Division

---

[64] The position was reversed by the Courts and Legal Services Act 1990.

[65] s51(8) Supreme Court Act 1981

[66] RSC Ord 6 r2(1)

[67] See page 75

[68] See pages 68 to 69.

[69] RSC Ord 72

there are special courts dealing with matters such as the constitution and winding up of companies and bankruptcy. All these courts, as does the Chancery Division itself, have their own special procedure which is outside the scope of this book.

An action for damages, trespass or breach of contract would be commenced in the Queen's Bench Division by the issue of a *writ*. This is equivalent to the county court summons. It has to be served on the defendant by the plaintiff rather than the court though. Service can be effected by post. If the defendant does not respond and give notice of an intention to defend within 14 days of service the plaintiff can *enter judgement*[70]. This involves sending the original writ, an affidavit confirming that it was served and the form requesting judgement to the court office. If a specific sum of money- known as *liquidated damages*- as will be the case in an action for a debt, is claimed a final judgement will be entered. However if the amount of damages is at large- *unliquidated*-, as it will be in an accident case, there will have to be another hearing for these to be assessed[71].

A default judgement can be set aside on the application of the defendant in much the same way as it can in the county court. Much of the subsequent procedure is similar to that in the county court. There are automatic directions only in a claim for damages for personal injury actions[72]. These are similar to the county court directions[73] but do not at the time of writing include any provision for automatic striking out in default of a request for a trial date. If the matter is retained in the High Court there will be virtually no difference between the procedure at trial and that which would have been followed had it been in the county court.

In the Queen's Bench Division, the court does not retain all the papers relating to the case. It is up to the parties to keep their own files.

A High Court action is listed for trial as a result of the plaintiff applying to have it *set down*[74]. This is done by him or his solicitors lodging two copies of the pleadings at the court office along with the

---

[70] RSC Ord 13
[71] RSC Ord 37
[72] RSC Ord 25 r8
[73] See pages 48 to 53.
[74] RSC Ord 34

form of request. In these papers must also be a statement of how much he believes the claim to be worth if it succeeds. The court may, in the light of that statement, order a hearing to investigate whether the trial should be in the county court or the High Court.

8. SPECIAL CASES

Injunctions

An *injunction* is an order by the court requiring someone to do something or stop doing it. In a case where it is alleged that someone has, for instance, trespassed on land in the past it is usual to also seek an injunction prohibiting them from doing so again in the future. The restraint of libellous newspaper articles, preventing unlawful picketing and copyright infringements are all examples of matters injunctions could be sought in respect of.

A final injunction will be considered at trial along with and in much the same way as a claim for damages.

It has recently been held that the small claims court has the power to order an injunction. The decision was made in a case where the judge thought it appropriate to order a landlord to carry out housing repairs[75].

Interlocutory Injunctions

Sometimes the obtaining of an injunction is a matter of urgency and the plaintiff cannot wait until the matter would be ready for trial to obtain his injunction. In that case the court will consider an *interlocutory injunction*, which will give the plaintiff his remedy until trial when the matter can be considered properly. In extreme cases this sort of injunction can be obtained *ex parte*, which is without the defendant being told of the application until after it is made. This is particularly appropriate in cases where if the defendant knew of the application, he would probably take steps to frustrate it. This is so in respect of *Mareva* and *Anton Pillar* orders, which are discussed in the following section.

Injunctions are granted most frequently in cases of domestic violence.

---

[75] *Joyce v Liverpool City Council* (1995) *The Times* 2 May

Where this is alleged the court can make an order requiring the man[76] to desist from violence, this is known as a *non-molestation* order. He can also be required to leave any home he was hearing with his wife or girlfriend, even if he is the sole owner of it, an *"ouster"*.[77] In only the most extreme cases will a court make an *ex parte* ouster. The procedure, outside the scope of this book, used in respect of these injunctions is different from that followed for general injunctions which are discussed below. Often they are obtained ancillary to a divorce petition.

In considering whether to grant an injunction at trial the court will apply normal legal principles in deciding whether the plaintiff is entitled to it. However the injunction is an *equitable remedy*, which means the court has a discretion whether or not to grant it, even if the plaintiff has made out a legal right to it. Where the plaintiff has behaved badly in relation to the subject matter of his application, he may be deprived of his injunction by the court exercising that discretion against him. For instance, in a claim aimed to prevent a construction company from swinging its crane over the plaintiff's land, the injunction was not granted in the terms sought. The plaintiff's only motive in seeking the order was to extract money from the defendant in exchange for permitting him to do this, despite having already been offered a reasonable payment. The use of the crane caused the plaintiff virtually no loss or inconvenience and the court considered its behaviour "inequitable"[78].

Where an interlocutory injunction is sought, the court will only be able to investigate the merits of the claim, to the extent of deciding that the plaintiff's case is at least arguable[79]. If it is, the injunction will then be granted if it would be more convenient than not to do so. If the injunction is found eventually to have been wrongly granted, the plaintiff will have to pay compensation to the defendant for any loss he suffered as a result of it. The plaintiff's ability to pay such damages and the defendant's to pay damages to compensate for loss caused by carrying

---

[76] It almost invariably is a man, though the jurisdiction can of course be used against either sex.

[77] The Domestic Violence and Matrimonial Proceedings Act 1976 and the Matrimonial Homes Act 1983

[78] *Woolerton & Wilson Ltd v Costain Ltd [1970] 1 WLR 411*

[79] See *American Cyanamid v Ethicon* [1975] AC 396, which has been considered in countless cases since.

on the activity are taken into account, as is whether more damage would be done to the plaintiff by refusing the injunction than would be done to the defendant by granting it. Normally however if the injunction would be a restraint on freedom of speech it will not be granted, if there is any possibility that what the defendant has said can be justified. An instance of this arose after a Mr Bigg was unhappy with the results when he painted his house, and the paint manufacturer refused him a refund. Mr Bigg wrote on the house, located on London's busy South Circular Road, words to the effect that the manufacturer was responsible for the mess his house appeared to be in. Although the paint company claimed this was defamatory of them because the fault lay with the method of application rather than the quality of the paint, they were refused an injunction[80].

An interlocutory injunction should be sought by the use of the normal county court application form. This should be supported by an application setting out the grounds on which the injunction is sought. Normally the judge will expect the party obtaining the injunction to draft it, though he should be prepared to give litigants in person assistance with this. If the defendant is prepared to consent to an injunction the judge may well ask him to make a formal undertaking to the court rather than grant an injunction.

In cases of extreme urgency the party seeking an injunction should arrive at court prepared to explain to the judge what the situation in respect of which he requires an injunction is. He should write out as many of the relevant facts as possible in an affidavit. I have never heard of an unrepresented party getting an injunction in this way, although there is in theory why it should not be done. If an injunction is granted *ex parte* the party obtaining it will have to give undertakings to bring his paper work into proper order within twenty-four hours or so. Notice of the injunction will have to be served on the defendant. If the situation between the parties has become so heated it is necessary to seek an injunction of this sort, it is advisable to appoint a professional enquiry agent to effect service. The court office will be able to provide suitable names and telephone numbers.

In the most urgent cases of all, it is possible to obtain an injunction

---

[80] *Bestobell Paints v Bigg* [1975] FSR 421

when the court is closed from a judge at his home. Sometimes this can be done over the telephone, sometimes it will be necessary to visit the judge. It is even less likely that an injunction could be obtained in this way by a litigant in person. Lawyers, particularly barristers, are familiar with the protocol involved in interrupting a judge at home. Legal aid, contrary to the normal rule, can be obtained retrospectively in a suitable emergency case.

Enforcing injunctions

When an injunction of any sort is granted or an undertaking given to the court, a breach of it can result in the offender being *committed* (sent) to prison. This process is set in motion by the plaintiff making an application. Usually an actual prison sentence would only be imposed for the most serious or repeated breaches. Other punishments available are suspended prison sentences and fines.

Mareva's and *Anton Piller's*

The *Mareva*[81] and *Anton Piller*[82] orders are two of the courts' most drastic remedies[83]. It is inconceivable that they would ever be granted to a litigant in person. Indeed the essence of the *Anton Piller* is actions that will be taken by a responsible solicitor acting for the plaintiff. With a few limited exceptions they can only be granted by the High Court.

The *Mareva* injunction involves a freezing of a person's assets pending the resolution of a claim against him. It is most frequently granted where the proposed defendant is living abroad, and so is more likely to be able to put his money where it will be difficult to enforce a judgement against him. The application is usually made at the same time as the claim is commenced. Its value will be lost if the order does not come as a

---

[81] After *Mareva Compania Naviera v International Bulk Carriers* [1979] 2 Lloyd's Rep 509, where such an order was first granted.

[82] Similarly after *Anton Piller v Manufacturing Processes Ltd* [1976] Ch 55.

[83] Memorably once described as the "nuclear weapons of the law- without the four minute warning".

surprise to the person against whom it is directed. Usually it will cause his bank accounts to be frozen to the extent of the claim against him, though he will be allowed enough for his reasonable living expenses. An unusual example of a *Mareva* injunction was where a man was killed in an accident involving a Nigerian company's aeroplane. When that aeroplane was in England his widow obtained an order preventing the company from taking it away again until her claim was settled. That way she could if necessary enforce her judgement by forcing a sale of the aeroplane and keeping the proceeds[84].

An *Anton Piller* order is normally made in circumstances where there is evidence to suggest the infringement of a trade mark or copyright. It is frequently used against the distributors of fake watches bearing reputable marks such as "Rolex", or of pirated videos or computer software. This sort of order is also best obtained before the action has begun. It enables the applicant's solicitor to raid the premises where the infringement is carried on and seize any offending items he finds there. He can also require any person on those premises to answer questions about those articles, who they were supplied by and to whom they were going to be sold. A similar order can also be obtained to obtain evidence in other sorts of cases if there is a strong likelihood that it would be destroyed, if the person in whose possession it is knew of the claim. In executing such an order physical force must not be used, but if the person against whom it is directed does not comply he will be in contempt of court.

A person against whom a *Mareva*, *Anton Piller* or any *ex parte* order is made has the right to go to the court and ask for it to be discharged or varied.

Children

An action on behalf of a person under 18 or a mental patient (in the strict sense of the word) has to be brought by his *next friend*. An action against such person is brought against a *guardian ad litem*. In practice most action brought by children are for injuries suffered in accidents, most against children are in connection with their interests under a will

---

[84] *Allen v Jambo Holdings* [1980] 1 WLR 1252

or trust or in care proceedings rather than as a result of some alleged wrong-doing on their part.

Where a claim is brought on behalf of a child, any settlement has to be approved by the court[85]. This applies even if a compromise was reached before the action commenced. An application should be made to the county court for approval. The child's parents would be well advised to instruct a solicitor to do this. The defendant or his insurer should agree to pay for this on top of the damages. If no such approval is obtained from the court, the child is not bound by the settlement and can start an action in respect of his injuries at any time until the expiry of the three year limitation period, which won't start to run against him until three years after his eighteenth birthday[86].

The purpose of this requirement is to protect a child from the possibility that someone would agree an inadequate settlement on his behalf and be in some way rewarded by the defendant for doing so. In many ways a child is more vulnerable to this happening if he is represented by a solicitor. The solicitor is entitled to have his costs paid by the defendant. There might be a temptation to accept a sma'ler amount of damages in exchange for the defendant not arguing about a somewhat inflated bill.

Companies and firms

A company, which will have "limited" or "plc" in its name, is a separate legal entity from its owners. A special procedure has to be gone through to form a company and it has to be registered at Companies House. The directors of a company cannot be sued for what the company does, hence *limited liability*. Most large businesses are companies. A firm or partnership is a group of people doing business together without having been incorporated as a company. Most firms are professional businesses, such as solicitors or accountants, whose controlling bodies do not allow their members to practice as limited companies. A partnership can sue or be sued in its own name, but the individual members remain liable, for their partners' actions as well as their own.

---

[85] CCR Ord 10 r10

[86] s28 Limitation Act 1980

Claims for possession of property

Claims by landlords who want to get rid of their tenants are one of the most frequent types of litigation in the county courts. Business premises are subject to a complicated code and distinctive procedure which are outside the scope of this book. However residential possession claims are a great deal simpler. Where possession is sought because an assured shorthold or similar tenancy has come to an end, there is a special form (N5A) which takes the place of the particulars of claim. In the latter case the court can, if there appears to be no defence after the tenant has been given an opportunity to state what his position is, make an order without there being a court hearing. If this simplified procedure is used, the court won't make an order for payment of rent arrears.

Where the rent arrears themselves are the reason for seeking possession, another form (N119) has to be used in the place of the particulars of claim. Except where there has been consistently more than three months' rent arrears, the court does not have to make a possession order for arrears. Lesser arrears or the tenant misbehaving in some other way merely gives the court a discretion to grant possession if the judge thinks it appropriate to do so. If the tenant's behaviour is not outrageous, usually a possession order will be suspended on the terms that the tenant pay off some of the arrears or that he does not repeat the misbehaviour.

Where the tenancy was granted before 15 January 1989, it tends to be even harder for the landlord to obtain possession. Tenants under such tenancies are more often "*sitting tenants*" giving them the right to remain there as long as they want. In addition they have the right to apply to the rent officer for a *fair rent* to be assessed on the property. Such a rent will inevitably be well below the market rent.

Boundary disputes

The essence of a boundary dispute is that one person is alleging another is trespassing on his land. The defence is that the land belongs to the person who has committed the alleged trespass. The court then has to decide to whom the land belongs. The person commencing the action should include in his particulars of claim a claim for a declaration that the disputed land is his. The defendant makes a counterclaim to the reverse effect. A large scale plan should be annexed to the particulars of claim showing precisely where the disputed land is.

Often the title deeds adduced by the owners of the adjoining properties will each show that the disputed land belongs to them. The court is then faced with a virtually impossible task of proving which should prevail. Each side should try to trace the title to their property back as far as possible. Sometimes old deeds shed light on the matter, but as often as not they are unclear. If one side has appropriated the land for the last twelve years and done so openly, that of itself is usually enough to give him a right to it whatever the deeds say[87].

Boundary disputes are a type of litigation that everybody whether representing themselves, paying lawyers privately or in receipt of legal aid, would be well advised to avoid. Often the claim is a "matter of principle". The value of the disputed land usually pales into insignificance in comparison with the legal fees incurred. There are cases where both parties- winner and loser- have had to sell up and move to smaller properties because of the expense of conducting litigation over a small strip of land!

Wills and trusts

Litigation involving wills and trusts has traditionally been conducted in the Chancery Division of the High Court. The county court does now have a jurisdiction if the total amount of the estate or the trust is less than £30,000. Such actions are often commenced by the *personal representatives*: the people who have a duty to administer the will, but who do not necessarily benefit from it. If they think a will is uncertain they will wish to seek the guidance of the court before they distribute the estate. Actions are sometimes brought under the Inheritance (Provision for Family and Dependents) Act 1975, which entitles a court to make a bequest to a dependent- including an adulterous lover- who has not benefitted from the deceased's will. This applies equally if he died without making a will so that his property would have been distributed according to the rules of *intestacy*.

---

[87] Limitation Act 1980 s15(2), see page 33.

These actions when commenced in the county court are known, somewhat inaccurately, as *fixed date actions*. Once the court would fix a date immediately upon the action being started. However now the procedures to be gone through are in many particulars similar to those where a money claim is involved.

Employment matters

Most disputes between employers and employees can be dealt with in an industrial tribunal. These tribunals have a separate and less formal procedure than the county courts. This procedure is outside the scope of this book. However one thing should be pointed out: that there is a time limit of three months from the date of the act complained of: for instance, in an unfair dismissal case, the dismissal itself. Whilst in some circumstances it may be possible to extend this period, mere ignorance of the right to bring a claim is not usually sufficient. The largely self-explanatory forms for making an application to an industrial tribunal can be obtained from any Industrial Tribunal Office[88].

An employee of course has the right to be paid wages for the work he does in accordance with his contract. If an employer fails to pay these he can bring a claim for them in the industrial tribunal[89].

An employee also has rights not be *wrongly dismissed* or *unfairly dismissed*. A wrongful dismissal is one that is in breach of the employee's contractual terms. There is an implied term in a contract of employment that arises after the employee has worked for one month, that he will be given at least one week's notice[90]. After he has worked two years he is entitled to one weeks' notice for each year he has worked up to a maximum of twelve. Often contracts of employment provide for a longer notice period. Normally an employer can dismiss an employee without giving notice so long as he pays him wages in lieu of notice. If however the employee is guilty of gross misconduct, such

---

[88] There is one at 19 Woburn Place, London WC1H 0LU, tel: 0171 273 3000.
[89] s5 Wages Act 1986
[90] s49 Employment Protection (Consolidation) Act 1978. See page 107 for an explanation as to how terms are implied into contracts.

as stealing from his employer or assaulting a workmate, he may be dismissed without notice or wages in lieu. Since July 1994 wrongful dismissal claims can be brought in the industrial tribunal as well as the county court[91].

Normally faced with a choice between the industrial tribunal and the more legalistic approach of the county court a litigant in person would be better off in the former. On the other hand if legally represented, and in little doubt about the strength of his case there may be advantages in the county court: the fact that he is more likely to recover his legal costs in that court is one such advantage.

Unfair dismissal claims can only be brought by someone who has worked continuously for the employer for at least two years[92]. If such a claim is brought, the employer has to show that there was a fair reason[93], usually misconduct incompetence or redundancy, for the dismissal and the dismissal has to be fair in all the circumstances[94]. The latter part of that requirement largely means the employer is under an obligation to operate a fair procedure before sacking anyone, whatever their conduct.

A claim for unfair dismissal can be brought be someone who has been *constructively dismissed*[95]. This means that the employer has behaved in such a way towards the employee as to make it impossible for him to carry on working. Behaviour such as demoting a person or making repeatedly critical remarks about him may well lead to such a situation.

The usual remedy for unfair dismissal is the payment of compensation, but the industrial tribunal does have the power to order the employer to take back the dismissed employee. This power would only be exercised against a relatively large employer, who would have the resources to keep the person whose actions led to the employee claiming constructive dismissal apart from him after the reinstatement.

---

[91] s131 Employment Protection (Consolidation) Act 1978 (as amended)

[92] s64(1)(a) Employment Protection (Consolidation) Act 1978

[93] s57(2) Employment Protection (Consolidation) Act 1978

[94] s57(3) Employment Protection (Consolidation) Act 1978

[95] s55(2) (b) Employment Protection (Consolidation) Act 1978

Public authorities

A growth area for litigation in the last twenty years has been applications for *judicial review*. These are cases where someone is alleging a public authority, a local authority, a health authority or a government minister have acted improperly in exercising their powers. The procedure involved is complex and the actions can only be brought in the High Court. Only the most ambitious litigant in person would bring such an action. A solicitor would be unwise to tackle one unless he or at least a colleague who could help him had experience of this type of work.

The basic principle is that public authorities have to act within the law. The proceedings are normally brought in the name of the Crown "*ex parte*" the person whose application it really is. Usually the powers of public bodies are derived from Acts of Parliament and anything they purport to do in excess of those powers is illegal: *ultra vires* is the lawyers' term. In some circumstances a court or tribunal may also be subject to an application for judicial review if it has for instance purported to exercise a power it does not have. Other grounds on which the High Court may interfere with a decision are that the person making it was biased or acting in circumstances where there was a reasonable possibility that he might appear biased. A decision so unreasonable that no authority acting sensibly could have reached it may also be dealt with by way of judicial review. However the High Court will only entertain an action for judicial review after all the internal machinery of the body being reviewed has been used. If the body is prepared to consider an appeal that must be pursued before any claim is brought in the courts.

The most common types of judicial review applications are where the Home Secretary has exercised his powers under the immigration legislation to refuse admission or deport somebody and where a local authority has refused to rehouse somebody. It is sometimes used by senior civil servants in respect of employment matters. More striking examples of judicial review applications that have found their way into the news in recent years have been the challenge to the government's reluctance to introduce European Community directives giving women employment rights[96], the refusal of a health authority to fund the treatment of a child with leukaemia[97] and the Home Secretary's attempts to reduce the level of compensation payable to people who suffer criminal injuries[98].

---

[96] *R v Secretary of State for Employment ex parte the Equal Opportunities Commission* [1992] 1545 QBD

[97] R v Cambridgeshire Health Authority ex parte B [1995] 2 All ER 129

[98] *Council of Civil Service Unions v Minister for the Civil Service* [1984] 3 All ER 935

9. EVIDENCE

What evidence is

Evidence is the means by which a party to an action proves the facts that he wishes to rely upon. In the criminal courts there are very extensive rules about what evidence is and is not admissible. For instance, the fact that an accused person has previous convictions cannot normally be referred to. The reason for this strictness is that decisions of fact in criminal matters are usually made by people lacking in legal qualifications: lay magistrates or juries. There is a fear that they might attach undue weight to irrelevant matters, such as the bad character of a defendant. In civil matters, which are almost invariably tried by a professional judge, this fear is much less prevalent. Also in civil cases there is not the concern that an individual's sacrosanct right not to be found guilty of something he hasn't done might be violated. Accordingly in the civil courts evidence tends both in theory and practice to be much more freely admitted than it is in the criminal courts. However a party still cannot tell the court everything it thinks might help his case.

Hearsay

Normally, a witness can only give evidence of what he saw himself, not what someone else has told him. This is known as the *hearsay rule*. Although it is not always applied rigidly in civil cases than it is in the criminal courts but a party to civil litigation should presume that it is going to prevent him giving such evidence. It is by far the most prevalent reason for excluding evidence in civil cases. At the time of writing there are proposals before Parliament which may result in a considerable relaxation of this rule in civil proceedings.

The effect of the hearsay rule is not, as is sometimes imagined, to make inadmissible all evidence of conversations people have had. The rule can be summarised as making inadmissible out of court statements (whether written or oral) which are adduced to show the truth of their contents. One of the most famous illustrations of this comes from a criminal case[99]. There the defendant was accused of illegally possessing weapons. His defence was duress: that he had been threatened with death by terrorists if he did not keep the weapons as they wanted. The trial judge refused to allow him to call evidence of what the terrorists had supposedly said to him, on the basis that it was hearsay. This decision was overturned on appeal. What the defendant had been trying to establish by giving evidence about these statement was that they had been made and had affected what he believed: whether or not he actually would have been killed was not relevant for that purpose.

Exceptions to the hearsay rule

Excluded from the hearsay rule is anything that a party to the action has said that is against his own interests in the case. This again is best illustrated by thinking of criminal cases: people are often convicted as a result of *confessions*. The confession is an out of court statement that is hearsay: when the jury is told of its contents they are being asked to accept that the contents are true. It is only because of this exception that such confessions are admissible.

Thus suppose in Mr White's case (see page 9 for the facts) Ms Fawn had said, as drivers often do after such accidents, "Sorry, mate, just didn't see you". This is a statement against her interests in the context of establishing liability in the case, therefore it would be admissible.

Statements which are made in the heat of the moment by the people who participated in the incident are often also admissible. They are known as forming part of the *res gestae*, which means the event itself. Again the leading example is drawn from the criminal law[100]. There a man was attacked by two robbers whom he knew. Moments later he named them to the Police. He died before the matter came to trial. His statement to the Police was admitted on the basis that it was so closely tied up with his being robbed as to constitute part of the events rather than merely being a statement about it. The hypothetical, "I'm sorry, mate statement" would also be admitted on this basis. However the principle could be applied if someone else, who did not have a direct

---

[99] Subramaniam v Public Prosecutor [1956] 1 WLR 965
[100] *R v Andrews* [1987] AC 281

interest in the result had said it at the time. Ms Fawn's passenger might have said loudly to her just after she hit Mr White, "You didn't seem to see him, did you?" Evidence of this from someone who had overheard it would be admissible.

Admitting hearsay evidence

In civil cases the judge has a discretion to admit a statement even though it is hearsay. There is also a procedure which gives a person a right to admit a hearsay statement in some circumstances[101]. If a party wishes to rely on hearsay evidence at trial he can serve a notice, generally known a *Civil Evidence Act notice,* on the other side. This notice must specify who the maker of the statement is, the gist of what is said (if it is a written statement then it is best to attach the statement itself to the notice) and the circumstances in which the statement was made. The notice may also contain a reason why the witness cannot be called. Acceptable reasons are because he is now dead; is abroad; is too ill too attend court; is untraceable despite reasonable efforts having been made to find him; or he cannot now be expected to remember the events[102]. However after the passing of the proposed legislation referred to on page 77, it is likely that the party wishing to introduce such evidence will merely need to give the other "fair notice" of his intention to do so.

Under the present system, if one of this reasons is stated, that gives the party an automatic right to rely on the evidence in the statement. However the other party does have the right to challenge the reason. There is unlikely to be much dispute about whether someone is dead, but a claim that someone cannot be reasonably expected to remember events is much more subjective! Ultimately if the parties cannot agree, the court will have to adjudicate on whether or not the person should be called. Even if no reason for not calling the maker of the statement is given, the other party has to serve a counternotice within seven days if the evidence is not to be admissible in statement form. Disregarding oversights, a party would only fail to serve a counternotice if he had no objection to

---

[101] Provided for by the Civil Evidence Act 1968 and CCR Ord 20 rr14-24.
[102] CCR Ord 20 r17(5)

that evidence because it was something he was not disputing. A statement from the person Mr White was working for at the time of the accident confirming that Mr White lost the work he claims to have lost, might be accepted on this basis.

More often than not the court will consider experts' reports, even if they conflict, without the exerts needing to come to court. (The reports are strictly speaking hearsay, if the experts do not give their evidence at court.) It is for the parties to liaise and decide whether their actual attendance, which is likely to be expensive, can be dispensed with.

To be effective the Civil Evidence Act notice must be served on the court and the other side at least fourteen days before the trial. In practice they are best served at the same time as the other witness statements.

Even once the law changes to allow hearsay evidence to be admitted more freely than at present, it will still be advisable to call witnesses "live" whenever possible. Judges are schooled in the idea that the best evidence is that which they can actually hear first hand and will remain suspicious of anything brought before the court in any other way.

10. THE TRIAL

The listing of the case

Once a request has been sent to the court office for the case to be listed for trial, the parties should be notified of the date. Most courts will assign a specific date, however some operate on a *warned list* system. Precisely how this operates varies from court to court. Usually it means that the parties will be told about a week in advance of the first possible date that their case will come on. Usually that date can be any time within the following fortnight. Some courts at this point give a precise date, others wait right up until the day before the hearing before doing this. Such short notice is only appropriate for a simple case with few witnesses other than the parties themselves. Even courts which run warned lists will give fixed dates to appropriate cases. The most compelling reason for the fixing of a date is the attendance of expert witnesses who need to know in advance when they will be required to keep their diaries free. Less attention is paid to the convenience of solicitors or barristers. Courts take the view that if they are "double-booked" when the case is listed, replacements can easily be found. If there are dates a party would wish to avoid for any reason, he should let the court know as early as possible. It is administratively much easier to avoid fixing a case on a certain date than it is to alter it after it has been fixed.

The trial itself may be in front of a circuit judge or a district judge. If the amount claimed is over £5,000, it will usually be a circuit judge, if the claim is under £1,000 almost invariably it will be a district judge. For a county court claim not involving any complex question of law the chances of having a fair trial in front of a district judge are exactly the same as a circuit judge. There are a few judges of both tiers who are incompetent and a rather larger number who are gratuitously unpleasant, but the majority do a good and conscientious job.

Most county courts list a number of cases to start at the same time, particularly those in front of circuit judges. The justification for this is that a high proportion settle at the last moment or have to be adjourned for some reason and that often despite the apparent overloading everybody's case does get heard when it should. It is of paramount importance to the Lord Chancellor's Department that never a moment of a judge's time should be wasted. It is infinitely preferable in the Department's eyes to have several sets of litigants hanging around court corridors than it is to have an empty court room. A lot has been said and written about whether or not this is merely a manifestation of judicial self-importance. What it means for the litigant is that there is every likelihood of his case not being heard at the time or even the day when it is listed. Generally speaking district judge's lists are better managed, partly because many district judges are not too grand to take a part in managing them themselves, and long waits are less likely.

Rarer but far from unknown is for a person to turn up at court on the date notified by the court and find that his case has not been listed at all and that there is no judge available who could try it. In this situation, though not merely when a case is not dealt with because of an overloaded list, compensation for wasted legal costs may be payable by the Lord Chancellor's Department. The application for that is made by writing to the *circuit administrator's* office.

Agreeing the bundle of documents

In the week before the trial, or before the earliest possible date if the case is merely "warned", the plaintiff should prepare an *agreed bundle* of documents. This should include everything either side wants to rely on at the trial. It is not necessary for it to contain all the documents that were listed at discovery, nor should it include the correspondence between the parties unless this is of particular relevance. The particulars of claim and defence should be included as should any further and better particulars of these documents. It is unnecessary to include the request for further and better particulars as this should be repeated in a properly set out response. Interrogatories and affidavits in reply should be included as should the actual list of documents each side prepared at discovery.

Relevant correspondence between the parties should be included as should any documents that will actually be referred to in evidence. It is essential however that without prejudice letters, particularly anything that may contain admissions of liability, are omitted. Similarly if a payment into court has been made, notices or letters relating to that must also be left out. If a judge sees such material he may feel it is prejudicial to his ability to try the case and insist on adjourning it at the last minute. The party whose fault it was that he saw the material would inevitably be ordered to pay the wasted costs.

The parties should liaise with each other over the preparation of this bundle. There is no formal rule that it must be done by the plaintiff though in practice it usually is. If the defendant but not the plaintiff is represented, the defendant's solicitors may offer to prepare the bundle. The plaintiff, particularly if he does not have access to a photocopier, will normally be relieved to accept this offer. However he should remember that if he loses and has to pay the defendant's costs, these will be increased by the work involved in preparing bundles.

If the parties cannot agree on what should go in the bundle, one will have to prepare a supplemental bundle. The only justification for disagreement is that one side wants to include material that the other claims is inadmissible and should not be seen by the judge at all.

At least four copies of these bundles need to be prepared- one for the judge, one for witnesses in court and one for each side. Most solicitors will prepare at least one extra copy for themselves: so that one can go in their file and one be used by the advocate who will probably want to scribble over it. Copies of the bundle should be delivered to the other side and to the court as early as possible.

Language and appearance in court

District judges are addressed as "sir" or "madam"; circuit court judges as "your Honour" and High Court judges as "my Lord" or "my Lady". Barristers sometimes use linguistic contortions to avoid using the word "you" to a judge: "does your Honour have the papers?", "would your Lordship give me leave...". This should not be attempted by litigants in person. No judge should indeed take offence at merely being addressed as merely as "sir" or "madam"[103] by a litigant in person. Lawyers refer to each other in court as "my friend" or "my learned friend". Lay

---

[103] Do though get the gender correct, though I am sure I am not the only advocate to have suffered the embarrassment of calling a not particularly androgenous looking woman district judge "Sir"!

people should not use these terms and should when referring to a lawyer involved in the case talk of "Mr X" or "Ms Y".

When giving evidence about another person ideally that person should also be referred to as "Mr X" or "Ms Y". However if it is someone with whom the witness is on first name terms, describing him by a first-name is acceptable so long as it is clear who is being spoken of. Talking of "my neighbour" or "my friend" except when initially identifying who the person is, should be avoided. "My husband" or "my wife" however is acceptable: indeed referring to one's spouse as "Mr X" sounds most unattractive in any situation.

Barristers of course wear wigs and gown in courts. They also wear bands which are wide white flaps hanging down about three inches over the front of the shirts. Male barristers also have to wear wing collars. Solicitors wear gowns, bands and wing collars. Some solicitors started wearing wigs in court a few years ago. With all the humour and sense of proportion for which it is renowned the Bar Council[104] raised vociferous objection to this. Eventually the Lord Chief Justice intervened to say that solicitors were not permitted to do so. Full time circuit judges wear purple gowns, High Court judges red ones. District judges and part-time judges wear the same wigs and gowns as barristers.

There is little consensus on how lay-people attending court should dress. Many barristers always take a spare tie with them to the criminal courts to lend to clients, hoping it will give a good impression. People who possess a suit would probably be well-advised to wear it for court, though it would rarely be necessary to buy one specially for the occasion. Whatever clothes one would normally wear for work are probably suitable for court (unless of course one is a dustman or sewage engineer!). Loudness of attire is more likely to antagonise a judge than casualness, two tone shoes, ties with large pictures on them, ostentatious jewellery, bright green suits, clothes which reveal tattoos, and sunglasses will be the *bête noire* of some judge and are best avoided. Of course these things shouldn't matter, but judges are human and like everyone else have their prejudices. Most are able to put them aside when they are acting judicially, but it is somewhat fool-hardy to have absolute faith in their ability to do so.

---

[104] The barristers' trade union, which it would go to great lengths to avoid describing itself as.

Starting the trial

Trials follow a fairly standard pattern though sometimes it will be dealt with in a way that differs from the norm. For instance in a claim for damages that arise out of an accident, the judge may decide that it is best to consider whether the defendant is liable in respect of the accident at all. In such a case only once a decision has been made on liability should the question of the amount of damages be considered.

Where there is more than one plaintiff or defendant or a third party to the action, the procedure will have to be modified to accommodate this. Joint plaintiffs who are represented will invariably appear through the same advocate: they can only be plaintiffs if they are presenting the same case to the court, otherwise one would have to be a defendant. If they are not represented, the judge is likely to insist that one speaks for all of them, although they will of course all be able to give evidence.

Defendants are often separately represented though: they may have very different interests. If, for instance Mrs Green had sued the manufacturer of the washing machine as well as its retailer, they might blame each other for what went wrong and would need to be separately represented. Where defendants are separately represented each (or his lawyer) will take a turn at cross-examining the plaintiff's witnesses, and each will call his own evidence. The defendants' witnesses will be cross-examined by the other defendants before they are by the plaintiff.

A straight-forward trial commences with the plaintiff *opening* his case. This involves explaining to the judge what it is all about and referring him to all the relevant documents, including the pleadings. In opening a case one should try to be reasonably objective. When dealing with matters that are in dispute between the parties each side's position should be stated. An experienced advocate should be able to give an impression of neutrality whilst at the same time being totally dismissive of the other side's case. The depth one is expected to go into in opening depends largely upon the judge. One who has read the papers in advance will be largely conversant with the issues and require much less explaining than one who comes completely new to the case. Most lawyers find opening a case in front of judge who hasn't read the papers much easier than in front of one who has. A judge's ignorance is something the lawyer can take advantage of by steering him in the direction the lawyer wants him to go. Where the judge already has a fairly good picture he will only want the lawyer to fill in matter of details: often these will be the details the plaintiff's advocate would rather gloss over. If there are any questions on which there may be legal argument, the judge should be told of these during the opening, however detailed argument on law is usually left to the end of the case.

Examining and cross examining witnesses

After the opening is completed, and the defendant does not normally have any right of reply at this point, the plaintiff starts calling his witnesses. The first thing a witness will be asked to do is take an oath. Sometimes the assumption is made, for white people at least, that this should be on the New Testament. Anyone wishing to swear in another way or to *affirm* (make a solemn promise with no religious connotation to tell the truth) should make that clear. Court ushers sometimes ask for a note of witness' religions before a case starts. This of course is not out of unwarranted curiosity but so they can have the right prompt card and holy book available when the time comes for that witness to take the oath.

After the oath has been taken the witness should provide his name and address to the court. Usually the written statement of a witness' evidence will stand as the main part of his evidence: what he wishes to tell the court, known as *evidence in chief*. If for some reason no witness statements have been prepared, this evidence might be elicited by that person's lawyer asking him questions. These questions must not be *leading*. People often refer to a "leading question" when they mean one that is important or invites a revealing answer. That is a slight misnomer. What the expression means in court is a question that invites a specific answer.

An example from Mr White's case might be:

> **Lawyer: Were you on the pedestrian crossing when you were hit by the car?**

A corrected version of this is:

> **Where were you when you were hit by the car?**

Any reference in a question to Mr White being hit by a car would itself be leading if it were in dispute that he had been hit. Strictly speaking if a person is giving evidence in chief without a lawyer to assist by asking questions, he will not be allowed to read from a prepared statement. Some judges will relax this rule. Notes that were made when the incident was reasonably fresh in the mind of the maker can however be used, whether or not the witness has made a formal written statement and whether or not he will be assisted by a lawyer. Permission to refer to any written material should be sought from the judge.

After the judge has received the witness's evidence in chief, whether by means of the judge reading a pre-prepared statement, the witness being taken through his evidence by a lawyer or by making his own statement from the witness box, the witness will be *cross-examined* by the other side. Cross examination is one of the most difficult tasks of the advocate. Many experienced lawyers have problems doing it successfully. However things are portrayed in television court room dramas, this is a process that very rarely results in the witness saying that his evidence has hitherto been a pack of lies! The first point to be remembered about cross examination is that it can consist only of questions. Most litigants in person when asked to cross-examine someone immediately start telling the court their own side of the story, which is not allowed. However cross-examination is not in fact very different from that. The cross-examiner should make it clear by questions to the witness which parts of his evidence are and are not accepted. The simplest form of cross-examination is to ask a witness, "Is this not true...?" setting out one's own version of the facts. A litigant in person cannot reasonably be expected to cross-examine in any more sophisticated manner than this. In some circumstances it will be possible to lay traps for the witness, but this is remarkably difficult to do successfully even for the professional advocate. If there are matters in a witness's evidence which are not challenged in cross-examination, it will be presumed that those matters are accepted by the defendant. Of course often things are not challenged due to an oversight rather than because they are actually accepted. Usually when the defendant or his witnesses give evidence, the plaintiff's lawyers will point out if anything is said that is inconsistent with what was said on behalf of the plaintiff but which was not put in cross-examination. If the matter was not put because in cross-examination because the defendant's lawyer had no knowledge of it, then the court may well infer this is because that witness had only just invented it. On the other hand if it is in a statement prepared for the defendant's advocate, he has to say so and admit to having overlooked it. This is mildly embarrassing for him but makes it clear that it cannot reflect adversely on his client. If it is a matter of importance that has not been put, whether due to an oversight or otherwise, it may be necessary to recall that witness to enable him to comment further upon it.

Cross-examination can be about anything the cross-examiner wishes to bring up so long as it is relevant to the case, it need not merely relate to matters that were dealt with in evidence in chief. Leading questions are allowed in cross-examination. However those which assume a state of affairs which are not agreed by the witness are not. The often cited example of such a question is, "When did you stop beating your wife?" This would only be asked of a witness who admitted having beaten his wife in the past but claimed to have now stopped doing so. Asking it of anyone else would be improper as it could only be answered by someone who had been beating his wife.

After cross-examination, there comes *re-examination*. This enables the party who has just been cross-examined to clear up any matters that may have arisen in the course of that cross-examination. Often it is also used by advocates to ask questions they overlooked when conducting their examination in chief. Although not strictly speaking proper, at least without the judge's permission, few judges are likely to prevent a litigant in person doing this.

Each of the plaintiff's witnesses gives evidence in turn. Any statements of evidence that are admitted without the witness being called should be read to the court, although many judges will not want them to actually be read out loud. After finishing all this the plaintiff or his advocate will say to the judge words such as, "That is my case". It will then be the defendant's turn to present his case, which is done in the same way as the plaintiff's except of course it is the defendant who then examines witnesses in chief and the plaintiff who cross-examines them.

Closing the case

At the end of the defendant's case, it is the defendant who first makes the closing submissions. This should be a review of the facts of the case, and here any legal arguments that arises on the facts can be developed. If lawyers intended referring to decided cases as authority for any proposition they may be arguing they will normally make photo-copies of these authorities available to the other side and to the judge, or at least give sufficient notice of what these authorities are to enable them to get their own copies.

Sometimes when the defendant is about to make his closing submissions, the judge may say that he would rather hear from the plaintiff first. If both sides are represented, this is good news for the defendant. It is likely then that the judge has made up his mind in favour of the defendant and merely wants to hear the plaintiff's arguments for the sake of completeness. A judge must listen to everything relevant the side which loses has to say. If he did not he could be accused of deciding against that side without giving it a proper chance to present its case. On the other hand it doesn't much matter whether he hears everything the winner has to say. It is immensely frustrating of course for an advocate who has thought up what he believes to be a brilliant and innovative argument to support his case, not to have the opportunity of telling the court about that argument! However if the judge can decide in his favour without hearing from him, he can have no legitimate complaint: the courts are not debating chambers to hear brilliant arguments for their own sake. Sometimes however if the plaintiff is represented and the defendant not, the judge will want to hear from the plaintiff's lawyer first because he believes he will get more help from him particularly on the legal issues in the case. The defendant will be given a full opportunity in due course to have his say but if it is a case where he hasn't been able to fully understand the legal issues it is unlikely he will be very effective in persuading the judge to change his mind.

The judgement

After hearing all the evidence and argument the judge will then make a decision. In most cases he will do that immediately after the end of the parties' closing submissions, taking perhaps a few minutes outside court to reflect. In the most complicated cases he may feel unable to give judgement on the same day as the case finishes and instead ask the parties to come back the next day or even at a date some time into the future. In all but the simplest of cases he will have to give detailed reasons to support the conclusion he has come to. Usually a tape recorder will be playing while he gives judgement. This will be so that if an appeal is necessary there will be a proper record of what he has said that the Court of Appeal can consider in due course. It is important to take a note of the judgement as it is being given. Unless one is a trained short-hand writer, it will not be possible to get down everything that is said. However writing fast one should be able to get the gist of it. For no sensible reason other than protecting the court transcriber's monopoly, litigants and lawyers are not allowed to make their own tape recordings of judgements.

Where a money sum has been awarded the judge should be asked to order interest on it. This will usually be at a simple (rather than compounded) rate of 8% per annum. Where the plaintiff knew precisely how much he was claiming, for instance where he had been seeking to recover a debt, this should have been calculated in advance. Where the judge has had to assess the amount of damages, it will only be possible to calculate the amount after he has decided what the appropriate principal figure is. The judge will allow a few minutes for the calculation to be made and if possible agreed with the other side. A litigant hopeful of being awarded damages should remember to bring a calculator to court with him!

After judgement has been given there will be argument as to costs. (The principles on which a court makes costs orders are considered on pages 94 to 97.) However it is important for the winner not to overlook the need to ask the judge to make the order that is sought: even somebody who has represented himself should be able to recover something. A party who has been legally aided will, whatever the outcome, ask for a *legal aid taxation*. This is merely an order enabling the Legal Aid Board to assess the amount that should be paid under the legal aid order. Very rarely does it have any bearing on the other party. If the other side has been represented by a barrister, the barrister may ask for a *certificate for counsel*. This has the effect that any assessment of costs will allow for the barrister's fees. After a full trial such a certificate is not necessary as they will be allowed automatically but is sometimes given anyway. After other hearings in the county court, including almost all in chambers (closed court) the certificate is necessary. A party against whom a costs order has been made has an interest in persuading the judge not to order such a certificate. In practice judges are reluctant to refuse one, most have been barristers themselves and they are sympathetic to the barrister's position. However objection should be raised if the matter was exceptionally simple. Sometimes a solicitor who has represented party will seek a *special allowance*. This enable him or his firm to recover more on taxation of fees. They are rarely given except where the solicitor has appeared in a complex matter against a barrister.

Considering an appeal

The first reaction the losing party usually has is that he wishes to appeal. In the majority of cases this is not a good idea. That unpalatable statement is made even more unpalatable by the fact that the less pleasant the judge's findings are for the loser the less likely it is that an appeal could succeed. Appeals are normally only viable on points of law. If the judge finds someone has not being telling the truth, the Court of Appeal won't interfere with that finding except in the most exceptional circumstances. If a judge actually went so far as to say, "I find myself unable to accept Mr Bloggs' evidence because he has a tattoo" that would be appealable, but judges generally have enough sense not to actually say that sort of thing. The Court of Appeal's attitude is that the judge had the chance to see and hear the witnesses and is in the best position to determine who was telling the truth. Only if a mistake of law is alleged, does an appeal have a realistic prospect of success.

If the court's decision involved less than £5,000, it will be necessary to obtain *leave to appeal* before actually appealing[105]. This can be requested from the judge who has just given judgement. He is only likely to grant leave if he has dealt with a difficult point of law and had doubts about whether he has necessarily come to the correct conclusion. Obtaining leave in this way does not oblige the person who gets it to actually appeal. If leave is not sought immediately after the hearing, an application can later be made to the judge. If it is refused an application for leave can be made to the Court of Appeal.

---

[105] County Court Appeals Order 1991, rule 2

The other basis on which an appeal can sometimes be made is if new evidence comes to light that could not have been available at the original hearing. A, perhaps slightly fanciful, example might be if Mr White had lost his case and someone approached him afterwards saying, "I saw your accident and made a video of it, which clearly shows you were on the pedestrian crossing when you were hit." If this is a complete stranger and there had been nothing that should have made Mr White aware that the accident had been videoed, then he could appeal.

A litigant in person who is minded to appeal on any basis should seek legal advice before doing so.

Hearings of small claims

Trials where the amount claimed is less than £1,000 (a figure which is likely to be increased by the end of 1995) will be conducted less formally but will follow the same pattern. They will be in a private room. A party may be represented by a lay advocate: which effectively means anybody he likes, a friend as well as an advice worker. If lawyers appear, they will not wear wigs and gowns. At the end of the case the judge may give reasons in a summary form. Orders for the payment of legal costs will not normally be made, though the if the plaintiff wins the amount of his court fee will usually be added onto what the defendant has to pay him.

11. COURT FEES AND LEGAL COSTS

Fees during the action

The county court charges fees at a number of stages of an action. The minimum fee on commencing an action (*the plaint fee*) is £10. If the claim is purely for money, it is 10% of the amount claimed (rounded up to the nearest 10p) for claims up to and including £600. If the claim is from £600 to £1000 it is £65, from £1,000 to £5,000 it is £70, over £5,000 it is £80. If other relief, such as an injunction, is claimed as well as money the same fees apply but are subject to a minimum of £50.

A defendant only has to pay anything if he makes a counterclaim greater than the original claim. Then he must pay the difference between the fee paid by the plaintiff and the fee for commencing his counterclaim if it had been an originating claim. Thus if the claim is for £500 and the Defendant counterclaims £700, he will have to pay £15: the fee for a £700 claim is £65, but the plaintiff will already have paid £50 to commence his £500 claim.

A further £50 is payable when a request is made to the court to list the matter for trial. This is not payable if the claim is for less than £1,000. £50 is also payable when appealing against any decision made in the course of the case.

Fees for enforcing a judgement

Enforcing judgement can be the most expensive part of the action. 15% of the amount of judgement is payable on the issue of warrant of execution, subject to a minimum of £10 and a maximum of £50. For the recovery of land the fee for the warrant is £50. 10% of the amount sought is payable (minimum £10, maximum £80) on the application for an attachment of earnings order. The fee for a charging order or garnishee order is £25.

Payment of fees and proposals for increase

People on income support are exempted from the court fees. There is a more general power to reduce or waive the fees on the ground that they would cause the person undue financial hardship. The court office should be able to advise about this. All cheques should be made payable to Her Majesty's Paymaster General (HMPG).

The fees charged by the court in many ways seem a bargain. The cost of a day of a judge's time not to mention all the back up staff and the use of the buildings is many times the highest possible court fee. However the courts do make money from the plaint fees in debt cases, where very little action, judicial or otherwise, is required by the court. Despite this the Lord Chancellor has proposed charging fees for court use that will go some way towards reflecting the actual cost. A figure of £200 per day, to be payable by the plaintiff has been suggested. There will be partial or full exemption for litigants on legal aid and possibly other people who could not afford to pay. At the time of writing these were still under discussion and it is not possible to say whether they actually will be implemented. The court offices should be able to provide details of the current position.

Legal costs

When a person wins the case, the court will normally make a *costs order* in that person's favour. This is directed primarily towards the costs of employing lawyers to fight the case. Where someone has won a case without a lawyer, he can claim a mere £8.25 per hour for his time in preparing the case. Whether or not a lawyer has been used, the landlord can claim out of pocket expenses for himself and witnesses and of course the court fee. If the costs are relatively small, as they should be if the case is decided at the first hearing, the judge will usually assess a figure when making the possession order. If they are substantial, the judge will order them to be subject to more detailed assessment, a process known as *taxation*. This is likely to result in the other side being ordered to pay considerably less than the litigant has to pay his own solicitor. The solicitor is entitled to his agreed fee regardless of the amount assessed. If no fee was agreed with the solicitor, the litigant is entitled to insist on solicitor's bill being assessed. The solicitor should provide details of how this can be done when he submits his bill. Assessment in this situation is done on a different basis to one that decides how much the other party has to pay, and the litigant is still likely to be out of pocket.

To give an example, suppose Mrs Green wins her claim (the facts are set out on page 9) and recovers more than £1,000 damages, having instructed a solicitor to act for her. Mr Blue fully contested the case and it went to a full trial which lasted a whole day. Mrs Green's solicitor's bill for that and all the preliminary work might well be £2,000. The court would make an order that Mr Blue pay those costs. However he would have the right to have those costs taxed. Taxation might result in Mr Blue only being required to pay £1,500 towards the £2,000 the Mrs Green would have to pay her own solicitors. If she thought her solicitors' bill was too much she could apply to have it assessed. It is unlikely that it would be reduced to anything like as low a figure as that which Mr Green would have to pay. It might well be assessed on this basis as £1,950. However unless the reduction obtained by Mrs Green were more than 20% of the bill, she would have to pay the costs-effectively for the solicitor's time- of the assessment: inevitably more than the £50 saved. A challenge to one's own solicitor's bill must be made within one month of it being rendered. However this time limit only runs once information about the procedure to make this challenge has been sent[106].

Taxation of costs between the parties is normally ordered on the *standard basis*. It is this basis which results in a difference between what the loser has to pay the winner and what the winner has to pay his own solicitor. However if one party has behaved particularly badly, perhaps having been found to have deliberately lied to the court, an order for taxation on the *indemnity basis* will be made. This has the effect that the loser will have to pay all of the winner's costs. A successful party who thinks that such an order is appropriate in his case should ask the judge to make the order.

Where costs are wasted by the fault of a solicitor, barrister, the court

---

[106] See the Solicitors' Remuneration Order 1972.

has a power to order that person to pay the wasted costs[107]. In fact this power is exercised very sparingly: only the worst faults, such as failing to turn up for a hearing, are likely to result in such an order being made.

Costs of interlocutory hearings

After trial a final costs order between the parties will be made. At interlocutory hearings the costs of those hearings will be considered. A number of orders are available to the court at this stage:

> *Plaintiff's (or defendant's) costs*: the party in whose favour the order is made, will get the costs of that hearing whatever the eventual outcome of the case. Most likely to be made where one party's fault, perhaps failing to comply with a time limit, has caused the hearing to be necessary;
> *Costs in cause*: whoever wins the case will get the costs of the hearing. Will be made where the hearing was inevitable or the parties were equally to blame for it being necessary;
> *Plaintiff's (or defendant's) costs in cause*: if the party in whose favour the order is made wins eventually wins, he will get his costs. Otherwise each side will pay his own. Usually made where one party is more to blame than the other for the hearing being necessary but not entirely so;
> *Costs reserved*: the decision on the costs of this hearing is to be deferred until a later hearing or trial. Will be made when the judge feels he doesn't have enough information to make a decision at this stage. If the costs of that hearing are not specifically dealt with when the judge makes his decision on costs at trial, they will be treated as *costs in cause*.
> *No order for costs*: each side will pay their own costs of this hearing. Likely to be made where each side is at fault in making the hearing necessary.

Often defendants against whom costs orders are made do not pay them.

---

[107] s51 Supreme Court Act 1981

This is particularly so in possession cases where the action may have been brought despite the fact the plaintiff knows the defendant has no money. If the losing party has been granted legal aid, the court will usually make a costs order, but prohibit the winner from attempting to enforce it unless he obtains the court's permission to do so. This permission would only be granted where the other person's financial position has improved considerably since he was granted legal aid. It might be worthwhile applying for permission a few years later if the losing party had, say, been a student at the time of the court order, subsequently gets his qualification and obtains a good job. Such an application can be made in the six years following the making of the order. In practice this is rarely done if only because after litigation the parties do not usually keep in touch with other and the winner will not know what has happened to the loser!

12. ENFORCING A JUDGEMENT

Enforcement

Getting an order from the court is frequently the easier part for a plaintiff. More often than not the defendant will simply ignore it. If an injunction is granted that is more likely to be respected because the court has power to send the defendant to prison if he breaches it[108]. The defendant's ability to pay is something that should have been considered before the action was commenced and so a sensible plaintiff should have reasonable confidence in being able to obtain his money. Where there is a monetary judgement there are a number of ways by which a plaintiff can attempt to enforce it.

Attachment of earnings

The most effective method of enforcement is often an *attachment of earnings order*. This involves a sum towards the debt being deducted each week from the defendant's wages[109]. Obviously it can only work if the defendant is employed: money cannot be deducted from social security payments in this way and it is impractical to implement against someone who is self-employed. It can only be used in respect of debts over £50[110].

An application is made for the order using the standard county court application form. The defendant then has eight days to respond. If he does not pay the whole amount due, he has to complete a form, which will have been sent to him by the court along with the application, setting out his means. A failure to comply can, after a number of warnings from the court, result in imprisonment[111]. Once the form is

---

[108] See page 68.
[109] Attachment of Earnings Act 1971
[110] CCR Ord 27 r7
[111] CCR Ord 27 r7A(2)

completed it is considered by a court official who will determine what amount he thinks reasonable to have deducted from the defendant's wages. Both plaintiff and defendant have a right of appeal to the district judge against the amount of such an order, which will be considered at an oral hearing. The order will then be served on the defendant's employer who must make the deductions that have been determined so that they can be paid to the plaintiff. The employer is entitled to charge five pence for every deduction he makes[112].

Warrant of execution

An order for the bailiff to seize the defendant's goods is known as *a warrant of execution*. To obtain this warrant it is necessary to complete form N323. If it is known that the defendant has certain assets, such as a car, then it is advisable to make a note of the appropriate details, for instance the registration number and where it is usually parked, when completing this form. The application will be handed to the bailiff who in the fullness of time will call at the defendant's home. He will take *walking possession* of the defendant's goods. This means the defendant has to give a legally binding promise not to dispose of them without the bailiff's permission. If the debt is not paid within a time agreed with the bailiff, they may be taken and sold at public auction. Certain goods such as the defendant's "tools of his trade" are exempt from this process.

If the debt is more than £5,000 this means of enforcement has to be conducted in the High Court[113], where it is known as *fieri facias* or *"fi fa"*. This is then conducted by *sheriffs*, who generally are more efficient than bailiffs. Judgements of between £2,000 and £5,000 can also be enforced in the High Court if the plaintiff wishes and sometimes the more robust approach of sheriffs attracts plaintiffs who have obtained county court judgements to take enforcement action in the High Court. The form used is the High Court Practice Form 86.

---

[112] s7(4) Attachment of Earnings Act 1971

[113] Article 8, High Court and County Courts Jurisdiction Order 1991

Charging orders

Where the defendant owns his own home or other property, it may be feasible to obtain a *charging order* against him. Such an order has the effect that the debt becomes secured on the defendant's land in much the same way as a mortgage. Obtaining a charging order will not give the plaintiff priority over the rights of existing mortgagees. The procedure is one of the more complex methods of enforcement and is most appropriate for larger debts.

The application for such a charging order is made on county court form N86. An affidavit should accompany this form setting out details of the judgement in question, the land and the defendant's interest in it. An application has to be made to the land registry to register the application against the land. There will then be a hearing before the district judge, where if he is so minded, he will make a final order. Once the order has been made, the next step for the Plaintiff is to obtain an order for the sale of the land, so that the debt can be paid out of the proceeds. A whole new action needs to be commenced to achieve this.

Warrant of possession

In a possession action once that date has expired by which the tenant was ordered to leave, the landlord should obtain a *warrant of possession* from the court office. (It is not possible to obtain this in advance of that date in anticipation of the tenants not leaving when they ought to.) To obtain this warrant it is necessary to fill in form N325. The bailiff will normally then set a date in a few weeks time when the tenant will be evicted. He will visit the tenant first to give him warning of the date of eviction: it is pleasanter for everybody if the tenant leaves voluntarily rather than having to be physically evicted.

Bankruptcy

Perhaps the most drastic method of enforcement is seek to make the defendant bankrupt (if it is an individual) or wind it up (if it is a company). The procedure is outside the scope of this book. Whilst the consequence can be drastic for the defendant, it rarely profits the plaintiff significantly. The defendant's other creditors will be entitled to a *pro rata* share in his remaining assets: usually the proportion of the debt recoverable is a small one.

Oral examinations

An *oral examination* is not a method of enforcement in itself but a means to obtain information that will enable the plaintiff to enforce his judgement. This requires the defendant to attend before the court clerk so that he can be examined about his means[114]. The plaintiff or his solicitor may ask the defendant questions at this appointment such as, "Do you own a car?". Most county courts have standard form questions that will be asked of the defendant. A few clerks have enough imagination to supplement these with other that seem pertinent, but a plaintiff would be unwise to reply upon a court clerk showing such initiative. The examination is requested by the plaintiff completing form N316.

The court does have a power to order the costs of the plaintiff solicitor attending this examination to be added to the judgement. The other way of finding out about the defendant's means, and also in some cases his whereabouts, is to employ an enquiry agent. A good one will elicit considerable information. Reputable solicitors who employ such agents usually prefer to know as little as possible about their methods!

---

[114] CCR Ord 25 r3

13. ACCIDENT CASES

Negligence

The principles on which the courts decide who is to blame for an accident are fairly simple ones, which it does not take any great legal training to understand. The allegation made by a person claiming damages because of an accident is that the other person has been *negligent*, which is virtually synonymous with careless, and that that negligence caused the accident.

The majority of claims are based on road accidents and it is not normally necessary to allege anything more than in what ways it is said the party to blame was negligent. If that person has been convicted of an offence, perhaps careless or dangerous driving, arising out of the accident that conviction can be relied upon to prove the claim although it is not conclusive.

Sometimes there is a statutory duty on a person to take reasonable care for another. The Occupiers' Liability Acts 1957 and 1984, for instance, requires that a landowner takes such steps as are reasonable in all the circumstances to keep his premises safe. This duty can extent even to giving a trespasser, particularly a child trespasser, a right to sue the landowner if injured. The Highways Act 1980 may provide a claim against a local authority which has left a pothole in a pavement. The Factories Act 1961 often provide the basis for a claim when somebody is injured at work. Contrary to common perception, the Health and Safety at Work Act 1974 does not: it is a criminal statute not giving any civil rights to accident victims.

It may also be worthwhile briefly examining the theoretical basis of the law of negligence. Much of the English law governing this stems from the infamous case of the snail in the ginger beer[115]. The woman who drank the contaminated beer became ill as a result. It was argued on behalf of the manufacturers that they did not owe a *duty of care* to the woman and hence were not liable. However the House of Lords decided

---

[115] *Donoghue v Stevenson* [1932] AC 562, which was actually a Scottish case.

that such a duty was owed. They talked of the *neighbour principle*, which meant that anyone whom it was foreseeable would be adversely affected by the manufacturer's actions was owed a duty of care. This wide ranging principle has the effect that establishing a duty of care, at least in so far as the causing of physical damage and injury, if not economic loss is concerned, exists is rarely a practical problem.

It is the question of whether that duty has been breached, in other words, "Has the defendant actually been careless?" that is the issue at the heart of most accident cases. Sometimes a third issue arises, "Did the breach of duty cause the loss complained of?". This may be an issue in cases where negligence is alleged against a doctor. Suppose a patient dies whilst undergoing an operation that is performed negligently. For him- more strictly speaking of course, his estate- to be able to recover damages it will have to be shown that had the operation been carried out properly he would in fact have survived. This too does not tend to be an issue in any but a fraction of accident cases.

Road accident cases

Road accident cases are sometimes referred to by lawyers as *"running down"* claims even where the accident is a collision that didn't involve knocking anybody down or running them over. Where an accident occurs, liability is normally apportioned on the basis of whose negligence caused that accident. There are no hard and fast rules about what constitutes negligence. Mostly it is determined by common sense. A driver who hits another vehicle after jumping a traffic light is almost certainly to blame for the accident, as will be one who strikes a parked vehicle. Driving too fast is also likely to be an instance of negligence, though the courts will consider whether a speed was too fast in all the circumstances rather than merely in excess of a statutory speed limit.

In many accidents more than one person will be to blame. If the person who has suffered injury is partly to blame, his damages will be reduced in proportion to his blameworthiness: known as his *contributory negligence*. Thus if a car pulls out of a side turning against a give way sign into the path of another which hits him because its driver wasn't looking where he was going, both drivers' damages for injuries suffered will probably be reduced, perhaps by 50% each or 40% of one and 60%

of the other. However the passengers in those cars would not have been negligent and will be able to recover their damages in full against either driver. Another aspect of contributory negligence is if a person who was not wearing a seat belt suffers injury in an accident, his damages will be reduced by about 20% on the basis of contributory negligence if the injuries would have been substantially reduced by wearing a belt[116]. Getting into a car with a driver one knows to be drunk can also result in damages being reduced.

Vicarious liability

Where someone is driving (or doing anything else that creates liability) in the course of his employment it is normal to make the employer a defendant as well. This is on the basis of the principle known as *vicarious liability*. Where someone commits a wrong in the course of his work, his employer is liable for it along with the actual wrong-doer. If the employer accepts that the accident did occur in the course of the driver's work, then it may not be necessary to make the driver a party to the action at all. If however the employer claims the driver was off on, to use the time honoured phrase, *"a frolic of his own"* rather than working, they both should be sued.

Motor insurance and the Motor Insurers' Bureau

Drivers are- or at least should be- insured against liability to others resulting from road accidents. Since 1988 the obligation to insure has extended to damaging property as well as causing personal injuries. Where an accident has occurred, however it is the negligent driver not his insurance company who is primarily liable. Initial letters alleging liability should be addressed to the driver, with a suggestion that he might pass them on to his insurers. If he fails to respond and his insurance company is known, then it is probably worth writing to them anyway. However if nobody responds ultimately proceedings will be issued against the driver. Even if the insurance company does respond,

---

[116] *Froom v Butcher* [1976] QB 286

if proceedings are necessary they will be brought with the driver and/or his employer as the defendant rather than the insurance company.

Where the driver is uninsured, the *Motor Insurers' Bureau* (the MIB) will meet most claims that the driver was liable for. The MIB has a theoretical right to recover these damages from the uninsured driver. In the vast majority of cases, the uninsured driver has very few assets against which anything can be recovered. The Bureau is funded by a levy on all motor insurance companies: ultimately by the premiums of those people who do pay their insurance.

The MIB will not pay the first £175 for damage to property nor for any such damage in excess of £250,000[117]. If the driver cannot be traced, either because it was a hit or run accident or he gave a false name and address, then the MIB will only pay damages for personal injury, not for damage to property.

If the driver is known, he should be sued in the usual way, but the MIB has to be given notice of the proceedings within a week of their being issued[118]. Normally the MIB will then take over conducting the proceedings in the same way as it would if it were the actual insurer of that driver. Sometimes it will nominate an insurance company to do that job on its behalf.

In the case of an untraced driver the procedure is different. The MIB cannot actually be sued. Instead it should be notified of all the relevant circumstances. It will then, in an appropriate case, make an offer to pay compensation calculated on the same principles as a court would have applied for the personal injuries suffered. If the person making the claim is dissatisfied with the decision of the MIB on either liability or quantum, he can apply for arbitration by a QC appointed by the MIB[119]. Legal costs that can be paid by the MIB when a claim is made against an uninsured driver are limited to a nominal amount.

---

[117] Clause 2 of the Motors Insurers' Bureau Agreement, of 21 December 1988
[118] Clause 5 of that Agreement
[119] Clause 11 of the Agreement

Damages for accident victims

Damages will be awarded to accident victims on two different basis: *general damages*, which compensate for the actually suffering and *special damages* which compensate for the financial loss. The general damages are assessed on the basis of *precedent*: what has been awarded for similar injuries in previous cases. Thus the loss of an eye will result in an award of about £20,000, the loss of a foot about £40,000. These are though only starting points. The amounts will be affected to an extent by the age (younger people will bear the affliction longer and hence get more), sex (women are presumed to suffer more in respect of disfigurement) and special characteristics of the injured person.

Special damages cover things like the replacement of clothing damaged in the accident and private medical treatment, and, most importantly earnings lost as a result of the accident. Where the plaintiff is off work for a relatively short period he will get his actual loss. Where he is permanently disabled he will get his annual net earning, known as the *multiplicand* times the number of years he might have carried on working (the *multiplier*). However this figure is constricted and even for a young person in very good health before the accident will not exceed 20.

14. CONTRACTS AND THE SALE OF GOODS

The most fertile ground for consumer disputes is the sale of defective goods. Closely allied to this is the supply of services. Both are done under *contracts*. A contract is basically any agreement between two people. It does not have to be in writing except for a few special cases, such as sales of land. The *express terms* of a contract are those which the parties have actually stated. In most contracts there will also be *implied terms*. These can be implied by custom or more importantly statute. When goods are sold there is an implied condition that the goods will be of satisfactory quality and fit for their purpose[120]. If they are sold by description, they must correspond with their description[121]; if they are sold by sample, the bulk must correspond with the sample[122]. Even more fundamentally the seller warrants that the goods are his property to sell[123]. (These rules do not apply to sales by auction.)

Where services are provided, whether by a plumber, a financial adviser or a solicitor[124] there is an implied term that they will be provided with reasonable care and skill[125] and within a reasonable time[126].

In consumer contracts it is not possible for a shop-keeper to escape his liability by giving the customer a form saying that no warranties are provided, or restricting his obligations to, say, a manufacturer's guarantee[127]. Even if the customer signs something saying that he accepts such a term, it will not be valid.

---

[120] s14 Sale of Goods Act 1979

[121] s13 Sale of Goods Act 1979

[122] s15 Sale of Goods Act 1979

[123] s12 Sale of Goods Act 1979

[124] But barristers are- anomalously- exempt: *Rondell v Worsley* [1969] 1 AC 191

[125] s13 Supply of Goods and Services Act 1982

[126] s14(2) Supply of Goods and Services Act 1982

[127] s6 Unfair Contract Terms Act 1977 and the Unfair Terms in Consumer Contracts Regulations 1994

Quite what is meant by "of satisfactory quality" is not always clear. Something which breaks down or falls to bits as soon as it is used will obviously not have met this requirement. On the other hand where it only does this after being used several times, the position will be much less certain.

"Fit for it purpose" usually has much the same meaning as satisfactory quality in relation to what the goods are normally used for. If however the customer makes it clear that he wishes to use the goods for some unusual purpose before completing the purchase, they have to be fit for that purpose as well. A standard construction pedal cycle is not usually used on mountain paths. If someone bought one and finds it buckles after being used that way, he would not normally have any cause for complaint. However if he made it clear to the salesman when he bought it that that was what he intended for, then having buckled it would not have been fit for that particular, if unusual, purpose.

If goods do not comply with these implied terms, the customer is entitled to his money back. There is no reason why he has to accept a replacement or a credit note, unless he wishes to. If he has incurred any expenditure in relation to the goods, for instance transporting them, both when he originally bought them and when returning them to the shop, he is entitled to that. In theory there is no obligation on him to even return the goods to the shop, though it might be a little hard to persuade the manager of a shoe shop to come and collect a pair of broken shoes and bring the refund money with him!

15 DEFAMATION

Probably the area of libel and slander attracts more litigants in person than any other area of substantial claims. Legal aid is not available for it and lawyers will, rightly, tend to advise people against becoming embroiled in this type of dispute. The legal fees involved tend to be astronomical, though those in the highly publicised cases involving newspapers and celebrities tend to be unnecessarily inflated by everybody using the most expensive counsel and solicitors they can find. Litigants in person of course do not incur legal costs of their own, but they do run the risk of being ordered to pay the other side's if they lose. However it is probably the area where litigants in person are most likely to be relatively successful. A Tory MP who is not a lawyer, Rupert Allason, claims over twenty victories in such cases representing himself.

Most defamation actions are based on libel, which is a statement in a permanent form. Initially this meant in writing, but now applies to anything recorded or broadcast. Slander applies to spoken words.

The law involved is relatively simple. A statement is defamatory if it would lower the person about whom it was made in the eyes of right thinking people. The classic case and example of this is the story about a Russian princess that she had been raped or seduced by Rasputin[128]. Although this did not involve any moral fault on her part it might (at least in the climate of the 1930's) encourage people to shun or avoid her. It was therefore defamatory.

Once it is established that a defamatory statement is made, its victim is normally entitled to damages unless its maker can establish a defence.

The most important (and obvious) of these potential defences is truth, or justification. The onus however is on the maker of the statement to show that it is true. In most defamation cases it is the truth or otherwise of the statement that is the main issue.

Other possible defences are that it is said in circumstances of *privilege*. The most well known of these is parliamentary privilege. An MP or Peer cannot be sued for what he says in Parliament however untruthful

---

[128] *Yousoupoff v Metro-Goldwyn-Mayer Pictures* (1934) TLR 581

or malicious he may have been. The same applies to anything said in court. A *qualified privilege* applies to things said by members of local authorities or other public bodies at meetings of those bodies. They have a privilege from being sued in defamation unless it can be shown they acted out of spite towards the person about whom the statement was made. Where the maker of the statement has a privilege that enables him to make it without being sued, the statement can be repeated by newspapers (and anyone else) without there being any danger of a defamation action.

In determining truthfulness, it is the substance of the statement that matters not the form in which it is made. So to write that, "Mr Jones said yesterday that Mr Brown is a liar and a thief" may well be literally true. However as its publication suggests that Mr Brown is a liar and a thief, the writer would be as liable for it as Mr Jones.

The other major defence is that of fair comment. This enables criticisms to be made in the public interest. To say a politician is incompetent would always be protected by this. So probably would saying his policies are dishonest. On the other hand saying that he was forwarding policies for personal gain would not be. By the same reasoning reviewers of plays, films, books and such like are also protected. Like some forms of privilege, this defence can be defeated if it can be shown that the comment was made maliciously.

A person who passes on a statement can also be liable. When newspapers are sued, often their printers and distributers are as well. This is usually motivated by the plaintiff's desire to cause damage to the newspaper by prejudicing its relationship with its suppliers and customers rather than because there is a genuine claim against these people.

It is even possible to defame someone completely accidentally. An example of this was a piece written about a fictional Artemus Jones, who was portrayed as a church warden from Peckham who had behaved somewhat inappropriately at a motor festival in Dieppe. Friends of an actual man called Artemus Jones read the article and believed it referred to him, although the writer of the piece had never in fact heard of him. The real Mr Jones successfully sued for libel[129]. However in cases of unintentional defamation an offer to publish a correction and apology

---

[129] *Hulton v Jones* [1910] AC 20. The real Mr Jones was needlesstosay a barrister!

may relieve the writer from any liability for damages[130].

Damages in defamation cases are high in comparison particularly with those awarded to accident victims. Few would deny it is anomalous that someone might be awarded several times more for being defamed than for losing a leg or seeing their child die. Probably these high awards are a consequence of the decision being made by a jury on whom there are few constraints of precedent. In personal injury accidents the decision is always made by a judge who will aim to keep his award in line with those made in previous similar cases.

Libel actions have to be commenced in the High Court. The usual rules about pleadings apply and the precise defamatory words must be set out in the statement of claim. If it is not clear from the words themselves why they were defamatory of the plaintiff, the special facts relied upon must also be set out. If the plaintiff believes the libel has been made or repeated deliberately, he may also be entitled to aggravated or exemplary damages to reflect this. These should be specifically claimed.

If a payment into court is made in settlement of a defamation action, the plaintiff may ask for leave to make a statement about this in open court. This enables the plaintiff to draw publicity to the vindication of his reputation that the payment represents.

Generally defamation actions are tried by a judge and jury. The judge will decide questions of law, such as whether a certain statement was made in circumstances which attracted privilege. The jury will try the questions of fact, including that of whether or not the statement was true.

---

[130] The Defamation Act 1952, s4

16. FURTHER READING

This book is of course as basic a guide to legal procedure as one will find. The definitive works on procedure are the *White Book* and *Green Book*, which contain complete guides to the High Court and county court receptively and are discussed on page 10. At £290 and £140 respectively they are beyond the budget of many who appear in the courts. The best value guide to the courts is *Civil Litigation* by John O'Hare and Robert N Hill, published by Longman. The sixth edition was published in 1993 and cost £26, but it is updated and the price increased every two or three years. The county court produces booklets designed to assist litigants in person at various stages of their cases, which are handed out free.

The best "serious" text books are Sweet & Maxwell's *Common Law Library*. Books which would assist in relation to areas covered in this Handbook include *Chitty on Contracts*, *Clerk & Lindsell on Torts*, *Charlesworth & Percy on Negligence* and *Benjamin on the Sale of Goods*. These range in price from £180 to £220. They are updated about every five years, though supplements for some are produced between editions. More affordable works produced primarily for law students include *Cheshire & Fifoot's Law of Contract*, *Winfield & Jolowicz on Tort* and *Furmston: Sale of Goods*. These cost between £15 and £30. Books on land law are something of a bargain. The two leading texts *Cheshire & Burn's Law of Real Property* and *Megarry & Wade: The Law of Real Property* are used by practitioners and students alike and cost under £30.

Halsbury's Law of England and *Halsbury's Statutes* contain text and annotated statutes respectively on every area of English law. They are each only available as complete sets of over fifty volumes for around £2,500. They tend to be fully renewed about once every fifteen years with annual supplements prepared between editions. The layout of these supplements can be rather hard to follow.

Acts of Parliament can also be found in *Current Law Statutes*. These like *Halsbury's Statutes* provide considerable annotation and explanation largely in the form of footnotes. *Current Law* is published in looseleaf form every few months and all the statutes are arranged chronologically unlike *Halsbury's* which is arranged by subject matter.

HMSO also of course publishes the Acts individually. These are available as soon as the legislation is passed, but do not have any commentary.

There are numerous legal periodicals. Some combine news with proper law reporting, like *The New Law Journal*, *The Solicitors' Journal*, *The Law Society Gazette*, which are published weekly and the monthly, radical *Legal Action*. Some like *The Lawyer* and *The Legal Times* do not contain authoritative law reports, but still manage to give details of leading cases in ways that should be reasonably comprehensible. All except the *Law Society Gazette* can be ordered through newsagents: only newsagents around the legal areas of big city are likely to actually stock them. They are not excessively priced.

More expensive are the "learned" journals[131], such as the *Modern Law Review* and *Cambridge Law Journal*. These contain articles written mainly by academic lawyers on their specialist areas of law.

Many public libraries contain reasonable collections of law books. Some local law society libraries are open to the public. Other possibilities for people wanting to conduct legal research include university libraries: some will admit the occasional member of the public as may the libraries of each of the Inns of Court in London, whose staff are normally extremely helpful. The Supreme Court Library in the Law Courts on the Strand in London is open to anyone actually conducting litigation in those courts, but the staff are unlikely to demand to see a copy of a writ before granting admission.

---

[131] Why this should be the case, as most do not even pay their contributors, is something of a mystery.

17. GLOSSARY

ABWOR: Assistance by way of representation a form of legal aid enabling a solicitor to represent a person at a specific court hearing: see also **legal aid**.

Alternative dispute resolution (ADR): The resolution of a dispute other than by going to court or arbitration. Usually involves a mediator trying to assist the parties in coming to a compromise.

Anton Piller **Order**: An order requiring a person or company to permit another to inspect his or its premises for items which might be used in evidence, and to answer questions relating to those items. Most frequently used in respect of copyright or trade mark infringements.

Arbitration: The determination of a dispute other than by a formal trial. Small claims (*q.v.*) in the county court (*q.v.*) are referred to arbitration by the court. Large commercial disputes are often dealt with by an independent arbitrator with the agreement of the parties who regard this as a more cost effective way of resolving them than going through the courts.

Calderbank **letter**: A letter making an offer of settlement which may be relied upon by the party sending it when the question of costs (*q.v.*) comes to be considered if the other party does not "beat" what is offered at the trial: see also **payment in, without prejudice**.

CCR: See **County Court Rules**.

Chambers: When the court is sitting in private with only the parties and their representatives being admitted. Also barristers refer to their offices as chambers.

Chancery Division: The Division of the High Court (*q.v.*) where disputes involving matters such as trusts, wills and the composition of companies are heard.

Circuit Judge: A full time judge who sits in the county court (*q.v.*) and Crown Court.

Common law: That branch of law connected with disputes involving generally torts (*q.v.*) and contracts (*q.v.*), rather than trusts.

Conditional fee: An agreement between a solicitor and his client under which the solicitor will only have to be paid if the case is won, but which enables him to charge an agreed uplift of up to 100% on his usual fees if it is won.

Contempt of court: An action in defiance of the court. Can either be *in the face of the court*, for instance being rude to the judge, or a deliberate breach of a court order such as an injunction (*q.v.*).

Contract: A legally binding agreement between two or more people.

Contributory negligence: Where someone has suffered an injury in an accident but has partly brought about the accident by his own carelessness.

Costs: The fees a person has to pay his solicitor. Often one side will be ordered to pay the others' costs at the end of a case. See also **taxation**.

Counsel: A barrister or barristers.

County court: A civil court, of which there is at least one in every large town, which deals with all but the biggest and most complex civil disputes.

County Court Rules: The rules which govern county court procedure. Usually abbreviated to CCR (*q.v.*). See also **Rules of the Supreme Court**.

Defendant: The person against whom a civil action is brought.

Discovery: The exchange by the parties of a list of the relevant documents they have or have had in their possession. See also **inspection**.

District judge: A judge who deals with interlocutory matters and minor trials in the county court (*q.v.*).

Ex parte: An application made by one party to the court in the absence of the other.

Equity: A body of law qualifying the common law (*q.v.*). Originally developed in the context of trusts. Is still sometimes used to deprive a person of a discretionary remedy such as an injunction (*q.v.*) if it would be inequitable to grant it. See also **Chancery Division**.

General Damages: Damages awarded to compensate for general suffering as opposed to specific financial loss: see also **special damages**.

Green form: Legal aid (*q.v.*) which can be granted relatively quickly and informally to enable a solicitor to give advice on a specific point: see also **legal aid**.

Hearsay: Evidence of something said or written not in court admitted to prove the fact that was so stated.

High Court: The court in which major civil disputes are heard. Along with the Court of Appeal it forms the Supreme Court.

Injunction: An order by the court requiring a party to do or refrain from doing something.

Inspection: The inspection by each party of his opponents' documents. See also **discovery**.

Interlocutory: An intermediate stage of court of court proceedings, before the trial.

Legal aid: Government funding to pay some or all of the legal fees incurred by relatively poor people in contesting litigation: see also **ABWOR, green form**.

Legal executive: A person who has passed the exams and met the other requirements set by the Institute of Legal Executives (ILEX). Normally employed by solicitors doing virtually the same work as a solicitor would.

Letter before action: The final letter threatening court proceedings before they are actually commenced.

Limitation Period: The period in which proceedings must be started after the cause of action as arisen. For most claims this is six years, though if damages for personal injury are sought it is only three.

Liquidated damages: Damages for a specific amount, usually referrable to a contract (*q.v.*) between the parties. In the county court a claim for the cost of repairing a vehicle damaged in an accident is also treated as being liquidated: see also **special damages**.

Litigant in person: A person conducting litigation without the formal assistance of lawyers.

Mareva Injunction: An order freezing the assets of a person pending the resolution of a claim against him.

Master: The "judge" who deals with most interlocutory (*q.v.*) matters in the High Court in London: see also **district judge**.

McKenzie Friend: A person who provides assistance to a litigant in person (*q.v.*) without actually representing them.

Plaintiff: The person who brings a civil action.

Payment in: A payment into court by the defendant (*q.v.*) as an offer of settlement. If the plaintiff (*q.v.*) does not obtain more by way of damages he will usually have to pay the defendant's costs from the time the payment in was made: see also *Calderbank* **letter**.

Pleadings: The documents in which the parties to litigation formally set out their respective cases, the most important being the plaintiff's particulars of claim (or statement of claim) and the defendant's defence.

Puisne judge: A judge of the High Court (*q.v.*).

RSC: See **Rules of the Supreme Court**.

Recorder: A part time circuit judge (*q.v.*).

Registrar: The old name, but sometimes still used, for a district judge (*q.v.*)

Rules of the Supreme Court: The rules which govern High Court procedure, and which may also apply in the county court. Usually abbreviated to RSC (*q.v.*). See also **County Court Rules**.

Small claims: Money claims in the county court (q.v.) for £1,000 or less: see also **arbitration**.

Special damages: Damages awarded to compensate for a specific financial loss: see also **general damages**.

Taxation: The assessment of the amount of costs (*q.v.*) payable.

Tort: A civil wrong, not arising out of any agreement or contract (*q.v.*) between the parties.

Vicarious liability: The liability one person bears for the act of another, particularly that of his employee.

"Without prejudice": A letter or other communication containing an offer to settle a case. This may not be shown to the judge deciding the case if no settlement results: see also *Calderbank* **letter**.

APPENDIX: THE WOOLF REPORT

Introduction

The Interim Stage of Lord Woolf's Report, *Access to Justice*, recommending an overhaul of the civil justice system was published on 16 June 1995. Lord Woolf is a member of the judicial House of Lords. Before his appointment to the bench he worked as treasury counsel, who although barristers in private practice, represent the government in the courts. He was as highly regarded amongst the legal profession as any senior judge, which no doubt was a factor in allocating the task of writing the report to him. Although he consulted widely before compiling his recommendations, the report ultimately was Lord Woolf's own rather than a committee effort.

The Report contains recommendations for a large number of reforms, some sweeping some minor, to the civil courts. Lord Woolf has not yet gone so far as to draft the rules that would implement the reforms. He wants to gauge the reaction to his proposals before doing so. Some of his proposals, particularly in relation to the small claims court, will be implemented quickly. Others will probably not be accepted at all, and some only after several years' consideration and amendment. However it is almost certain that the Report will have sufficient impact to amount to the biggest change to the civil justice system for decades. It will impact upon all who become involved in the courts, whether professionally or as litigants in person.

"Small" claims

The suggested reform likely to have the most immediate effect is that of increasing the small claims limit to £3,000. The Lord Chancellor has indicated that he intends to implement that in the autumn of 1995. Depending on the success of this system, consideration will be given to further raising it to £5,000.

Personal injury cases will however be outside this system. If Lord Woolf's proposal for a "fast track" system for claims between £3,000 and £10,000, is accepted all personal injury claims up to £10,000 will come within that. Until however that is dome the present arrangements for personal injury claims will remain unchanged; i.e. those under £1,000 will be dealt with as small claims, those over that amount as part of the main court process.

The district judge will be given a wider discretion to transfer complex claims outside the small claims system. Preliminary hearings for small claims will be abolished in all but the most exceptional circumstances. The court staff will be encouraged to clarify any matters of difficulty with the parties by writing or using the telephone. The parties will also in appropriate cases be encouraged to have their disputes settled by a consideration of the papers rather than an oral hearing.

The retail sector will be encouraged to develop its own ombudsman schemes similar to those now operated by a number of service industries. There will be systems enabling cases to be transferred between the courts and ombudsman systems and *vice versa*.

Litigants in person

One of the themes of Lord Woolf's proposals is the encouragement of litigants in person. This will partly be achieved by the increase in the small claims limit to £3,000, in which a party does not bear the risk of having to pay the other side's costs. The other changes, which do not involve any major upheaval, are also likely to be introduced soon.

A general direction will be given to judges to be of assistance to litigants in person. Most judges already are. Those that aren't probably do so as a result of their deep seated prejudice against non-lawyers appearing in courts. It is not realistic to expect such attitudes to change because a directive comes from the Lord Chancellor's Department telling judges to do so.

Legal aid in a limited form may be made available to assist litigants in person at various stages of their cases. This would seem to already be covered- at least for people of limited means- by "Green Form" legal aid. Citizens' Advice Bureaux may also be encouraged to set up in courts. Kiosks containing computer terminals capable of giving basic legal advice may be placed in court buildings. Lord Woolf sees this as a possible means by which little-used courts currently threatened with closure might be kept open. Other proposals include allowing litigants in person access to court libraries and providing private facilities for filling in forms. Mobile courts which will visit areas where there is not sufficient legal business to justify a permanent court may be introduced, probably having evening and weekend sessions for small cases.

The "fast-track" system

For claims between £3,000 and £10,000 and all personal injury claims Lord Woolf has proposed a "fast track" system. The features of this would be aimed towards reducing the parties' costs. There will be a discretion to transfer cases in or out of this "track", even if they are over or under the upper limit. The upper limit for this "track" may, if it proves successful, be increased to £15,000.

There would be fixed costs that could be awarded in one party's favour against the other. This would not prevent a solicitor charging his own client more than those costs, so long as the implications are clearly explained to the client when the litigation is commenced. At the moment where there are fixed scales of costs, the court has a discretion to allow more. Theoretically this discretion should only be operated in cases where there are exceptional circumstances justifying the uplift. Courts however are reasonably indulgent about this and frequently allow it on fairly flimsy grounds. Although Lord Woolf does not propose such a discretion, it is likely that any system will allow for an uplift for exceptionally difficult cases. The fixed costs are likely to be calculated with reference to the amount claimed. Appended to the report is the scale of fixed costs allowed in German courts. On a claim for £4,514 the lawyers fees allowed are £806, on one for £451,365 the amount increases considerably less than proportionately to £8,429. These are smaller amounts than English lawyers would normally charge, even for cases that settle before trial.

"Fast-track" cases will follow a set timetable with the trial taking place within 20 to 30 weeks of the commencement of the case. The present system of automatic directions in the county court should produce a similar effect, but frequently does not do so. It is difficult to see how delays can be prevented by the imposition of a rigid timetable. The idea is that as soon as a defence is served the parties will be given an indication of the week in which the trial is likely to be held, with a precise date being allocated at least eight weeks beforehand. Personal injury cases will probably take a little longer to bringing on for trial because of the delays that are usually caused by obtaining doctor's reports (which is not itself an inevitable state of affairs, but one which Lord Woolf has not proposed reforming).

Even less practical is the suggestion of restricting trials to three hours. The difficulties are obvious: the issues may be too complex to reduce to such a short period; how would the time be divided between the parties; some judges deal with cases more quickly than others; advocates might rely on the time limit as a reason for not putting information before the court that they were bound to disclose but which was against their clients' interests. Lord Woolf merely proposes that the time should be divided equally between the parties. Judgements will be given in a shorter form than at present. The judge will not be required to fully analyse issues of law. Lack of certainty about how the judge reached his conclusion is likely to lead more appeals though, and to prevent this judges will probably spell things out as clearly as they can whether or not actually required to do so. The judge will have a discretion to extend the hearing to a full day but anything more than that would- if the rigid timetabling proposed were actually introduced- throw the system into disarray. It is unlikely that this part of the proposal will be introduced in anything other than such a diluted form with so many exceptions as to make it virtually meaningless.

On the "fast track" system experts will not be allowed to give oral evidence. As a costs saving measure this obviously has a lot to commend it, but it too may not prove all that practical. A judge faced with one surveyor's report which says that repairs to a plaintiff's property would cost £10,000 to carry out and another that says £2,000 is sufficient is going to find it difficult to know which to prefer. What does he do? Accept the views of the surveyor with the more eminent qualifications? Accept the views of the surveyor whose report is better presented and more elegantly expressed? These solutions are obviously unsatisfactory. Lord Woolf talks of the possibility of court appointed experts being used either to provide the only evidence or to help the judge determine the conflicts between the parties' evidence. It is of course difficult to accept that the introduction of further personnel into the litigation system is likely to reduce costs!

When experts attend courts advocates and the judge will question them.

It is the responses to these questions that provide the most reliable means for the judge to determine which of them gives evidence that is to be preferred. Again it is likely that this proposal will be introduced in a form that is no more than an exhortation to the parties to agree on expert evidence, rather than an absolute prohibition on the judge's right to determine cases in the best possible way.

The "multi-track" system

Cases where over £10,000 is claimed will normally be entered onto the "multi-track". This will be the closest to the present system. One of the novel features of this system will be "case management conferences", supervised by a judge shortly after the defence is filed and a pre-trial review a few weeks before the trial. At each of these the parties will be required to give an estimate of the costs incurred so far and how much the total is likely to be if the matter does proceed to a full trial. The case management conference should be attended by the solicitor or barrister with conduct of the matter, and attendance at the pre-trial review by the advocate who will be presenting the case at trial will be compulsory. The litigant or someone authorised to act on his behalf will be required to attend both hearings. No doubt these hearings are intended partly as a means of enabling the judge to comment to the litigants on their lawyers' conduct: the resulting strife between client and lawyer may not prove conducive to disposing of the case quickly and cheaply. However the requirement that the litigant attend does seem designed to encourage settlement negotiations. Often lawyers at a preliminary hearing are confident that they could reach a reasonable compromise, but are unable to do so because they don't have any instructions from their clients.

On the other hand requiring the lawyer with conduct of the matter to attend is often pointless, particularly if it is not a case where a settlement is a realistic possibility. At these conferences the parties will have to state whether they have considered using Alternative Dispute Resolution (see page 15) and if not, justify their failure to do so. The insistence of the parties' attendance at these hearings is also somewhat at odds with a recommendation that for "procedural hearings" attendance will not be necessary if they can be conducted by telephone.

These preliminary hearings are in keeping with one of the main themes of the recommendations: that there should be a transfer in the management of litigation from the parties to the courts. Summary judgement for instance could be given by the court in favour of either the plaintiff or the defendant on the court's own initiative as well as on the application of a party.

Pleadings

A number of proposals, which apply equally to "fast-track" and "multi-track" cases, are made in respect of the pleadings (to be renamed *statement of case*) and similar documents that are used in litigation. The Report summarises what should go in such statements. These seem to basically be the same as what is included in pleadings at present. However leave to serve a reply (see page 44) will be necessary. Judges normally only grant leave to serve a document after seeing what is to be contained in it. Thus where a party's lawyers think a reply is necessary they will still have to spend the time drafting that although it may prove futile, then spend further time making an application to the court.

Lord Woolf says that statements of case should not be used as a means of parties concealing the lack of merit in a claim or a defence. The sentiment is noble, but lawyers who have become skilled in using the existing form of pleadings to do just that will be able to do exactly the same with these statements.

In "multi-track" cases the parties will be encouraged to produce a joint statement of issues in dispute, which will supersede their pleadings. Again time- and hence costs- will have to spent in preparing this.

Settlement

Offers of settlement will be encouraged. The rules will be amended to expand the circumstances in which *Calderbank* letters (see page 12) can be sent. For instance, a plaintiff in a case arising out of a road accident may make an offer to accept that he was 25% to blame for the accident. Unless the judge finds the plaintiff more to blame, the defendant would have to bear any costs that were incurred in relation to establishing liability. The present system of payments into court is eventually likely to be abolished.

Litigants who behave unreasonably will be subject to orders that they pay the others sides' costs immediately and on an indemnity basis (see page 95). Generally speaking litigants' unreasonable behaviour is in fact that of their solicitors. Ordering such costs against the litigants personally is likely to result in an increased number of claims for costs against solicitors. Such claims take time to resolve. They are usually left best until the end of the case. A serious dispute between a litigant and his solicitor is likely to result in him needing to instruct new solicitors, a process which inevitably delays the hearing of a case.

Discovery

In respect of discovery (see page 49) a party will be free to refuse to disclose documents on the grounds that full disclosure would involve voluminous documents. Discovery may then be restricted to those that can be located without undue difficulty and expense. The other party may seek an order for further discovery but that will only be granted if the judge thinks the benefit of ordering it outweighs the likely cost. The danger of a proposal of this sort is that it will make it much easier for a party to conceal documents that are adverse to its case, just as advocates may rely on time constraints to be less frank with the court than they should.

The court structure

Lord Woolf does not recommend the seemingly obvious reform of merging the High Court and county court, though they may eventually be governed by a single set of Rules. Probably underlying this is the need to retain an elite group of judges, which those who sit in the High Court are. Their status would be eroded by the introduction of a single tier of judiciary with the result that it would prove more difficult to attract the most able and highest paid lawyers to become judges.

However the distinction between the two courts will probably become less significant: the High Court will retain exclusive jurisdiction over *Mareva* and *Anton Piller* injunctions (see pages 68 to 69), judicial review (see page 75) and defamation actions. Litigants will be able to commence actions in any court, and it will be up to the court to see that it is allocated to the court that is appropriate in view of the amount and issues involved.

The reports talks of judges working in teams. Each case will be allocated to a judicial team and will only be dealt with by members of that team, though probably only "multi-track" cases will require active judicial intervention before trial. These teams will be managed by a master or district judge, i.e. the lowest levels of the judiciary. This could create friction between them and High Court and circuit judges, particularly the more established ones who might see it as a challenge to their autonomy even independence.

A judge known as the "Head of Civil Justice" will take responsibility for the whole of the system. The closest to that role at the moment is the Master of the Rolls, who has responsibility for the Civil Division of the Court of Appeal. However his remit does not extend to procedural matters in the lower courts. There is a judge in charge of each Division of the High Court: the Lord Chief Justice, the Vice Chancellor and the President of the Family Division. However the Lord Chief Justice tends to largely concentrate on his work in charge of the Criminal Division of the Court of Appeal, leaving the Queen's Bench Division, of which he is the nominal head, lacking an obvious overall authority.

The courts are presently divided into circuits: the South Eastern, Midland and Oxford, Wales and Chester, Western and Northern. Court administration and to an extent barristers' practices tend to be based around one particular circuit. These do not though particularly tie in with any other natural or administrative boundaries. The Report frequently refers to circuits without their seeming to have been any consideration about whether these should be abolished or rearranged.

INDEX

Official referees 62
Ombudsman schemes 16

Particulars of claim
    examples 34, 36-7, 38, 39
Payment into court 60-1
    trial bundle, and 82-3
Personal injury cases 37-8
    contributory negligence 102-3
    damages 106
    directions 63
    insurance 104-5
    interim payments 58
    negligence 102-3
    road accidents 102-3
    schedule of special damages 38
    under £50,000 62
    vicarious liability 104
    Woolf Report 120-1
Possesion actions 71
    enforcement 100
Pretrial review 53

Queen's counsel 26

Recorders 31
Reply 43
    Woolf Report 123
RSC see **Rules of the Supreme Court**
Rules of the Supreme Court 9-10

Sale of goods 107-8
Security for costs 59
Setting down
    county court 52-3
    example of letter requesting 52-3
    High Court 62-3
    small claims court 17
    directions 55
Slander see Defamation
Small claims
    hearing of 92
    proposals for reform 118
solicitors 24-26
    articled clerks 26-27
    bills 28
    complaints about 29-30

delay 53
    rights of audience 25, 29
    special allowance 91
    wigs and gowns 84
Solicitors' Complaints bureau 29-30
Striking out 57
    automatic in county court 33
    no cause of action 57
Summary judgement 55-6
    affidavit 56
    considerations 56

Trial bundle 82-3
Trusts 72-3

Vexatious litigants 23

White Book 10, 112 see also **Rules of the Supreme Court**
Wills 72-3
Without prejudice letters 12-13
    Calderbank letters 13
    examples 12, 13
    meaning 12
    trial bundle and 82-3
Witnesses
    examination of 86
Witness statements 51
    exchanging 52-3
Woolf Report
    Calderbank letters 123
    case management systems 122
    court structure 124-5
    discovery 124
    expert evidence 121-22
    "fast track" system 120-22
    litigants in person 119-20
    Lord Woolf 118
    "multi-track" system 122-3
    pleadings 123
    pre-trial reviews 122
    small claims 119-20
    time limits for trials 121
    timetables for litigation 120-1
    wasted costs 123-4
Writ 43, 63